PRACTICAL ADVICE, INSPIRATION, AND PROJECTS

CREATE YOUR *dream home* ON A BUDGET

DANIEL AND NOELL JETT

THOMAS NELSON
Since 1798

Create Your Dream Home on a Budget

© 2022 Daniel Jett and Noell Jett

Published in Nashville, Tennessee, by Thomas Nelson. Thomas Nelson is a registered trademark of HarperCollins Christian Publishing, Inc.

Photography by Leslie Brown Photography—Nashville, Tennessee.

Additional photography by Natalie Mathers with Mathers Photography, p. viii; Shutterstock/Belova Yulyja, p. 8; Shutterstock/Moha El-Jaw, p. 15; Shutterstock/Innalex, pp. 24; Shutterstock/oYOo, p. 25; Shutterstock/Followtheflow, p. 26 and 161; Shutterstock/Lapina, p. 29; Shutterstock/PixHound, p. 30; Shutterstock/united photo studio, p. 40 and 199; Shutterstock/Africa Studio, p. 142; Shutterstock/Pixel-Shot, p. 151; Shutterstock/TheCreativeBrigade, p. 154; Shutterstock/VanoVasaio, p. 171; Shutterstock/Breadmaker, p. 173; Shutterstock/Phovoir, p. 177; Shutterstock/Linda Rhodes, p. 182; Shutterstock/timltv, p. 199.

Thomas Nelson titles may be purchased in bulk for educational, business, fundraising, or sales promotional use. For information, please email SpecialMarkets@ThomasNelson.com.

Any internet addresses, phone numbers, or company or product information printed in this book are offered as a resource and are not intended in any way to be or to imply an endorsement by Thomas Nelson, nor does Thomas Nelson vouch for the existence, content, or services of these sites, phone numbers, companies, or products beyond the life of this book.

This book is intended to serve as inspiration and ideas for home building and renovation projects. It is not intended as a substitute for seeking either financial guidance or for legal advice pertaining to building codes in your area. The reader should consult construction professionals in matters relating to their construction or remodel, including obtaining appropriate permits. Also, it's vital to follow all safety instructions pertaining to each individual tool, as determined by the manufacturer guidelines. Failing to do so could result in serious injury or death.

Art direction: Tiffany Forrester
Interior design: Kristen Sasamoto

ISBN 978-1-4002-3077-8 (eBook)
ISBN 978-1-4002-3075-4 (HC)

Printed in China
22 23 24 25 26 RRD 10 9 8 7 6 5 4 3 2 1

To our children.
No matter what we accomplish, you are our greatest achievement.

CONTENTS

PART THREE: *Room-by-Room Guide*

JETT'S RESIDENCE

ST. AUGUSTINE,
FLORIDA

MARCH 22, 2018

CONSTRUCTION DOCUMENTS

S&A

PROJECT NO. P17205

INTRODUCTION

We found a paper in a box of memorabilia Daniel had written in high school that listed his top three goals for his life: get married, have lots of kids, and build his own home. Ten years after high school, we met, and as we fell in love, these quickly became *our* dream!

Over the next seven years, we focused on growing our contracting business, which centered on insurance work on water-damaged properties as well as kitchen and bathroom remodels, until we could afford to build our home. During that time, we also looked for land and spent hours perusing house plans.

One day, we were chatting about a lot for sale just up the road from us. Daniel mentioned that he had driven by it, and while that lot was not what we would want, there was a vacant lot at the very back of that road that he instantly loved—and knew I would too. It was located on a cul-de-sac, and three beautiful oak trees stood right in the center of it, immediately causing us to dream of swings hanging from their branches, our children happily playing in the shadows cast by their sweeping canopies. We searched the county appraiser's website to find the owner's information, hoping to draft them a letter to see if they would be interested in selling to our family. The very next day, Daniel called me and said he was right next to their home visiting a customer and wondered if I thought it would be a good idea to stop by and talk to the owners about their property. I told him they would either love him or shoot him, so he should talk quickly.

> I told him they would either love him or shoot him, so he should talk quickly.

brick
with key

SHE MADE HERSELF **A HOME**

RACHEL ASHWELL Couture Prairie AND FLEA MARKET FINDS

Ball
IDEAL

Turns out, the sweet elderly couple had purchased the land almost thirty years ago with the dream of building on it themselves, but it had never worked out. They loved the idea of a young family building their dream home on it and initially agreed to sell to us— then changed their minds. We went from being on cloud nine to feeling crushed. Pieces of land like this one are almost unheard of where we live in St. Augustine, Florida, where everything is high and dry. This had beautiful trees on it, was relatively close to town, and, most importantly, was not even five minutes from Daniel's parents.

However, we did not lose hope. We waited six months, then unbeknownst to me, Daniel reached back out to see if the landowners would reconsider. Surprisingly, they said yes! My birthday, which happens to fall on Christmas, was the following week, so, as one of my presents, he surprised me with a copy of the signed contract and a brick with a key attached to it, symbolizing the home he was going to build for me.

As excited as we were to finally begin this process, we had no idea what we were getting ourselves into and how our lives were about to change. We began finalizing our house plans as we attempted to secure financing and researched materials and subcontractors, trying to get all the pieces into place.

One night, while browsing the Architectural Designs website, we noticed they had added a client album featuring customers' homes. One housebuilder's description included a link to an Instagram account filled with construction pictures. Until then, I had only used Instagram to add filters to my photos and had never heard of "growing your platform" or social media marketing. However, I knew we were going to be doing a lot of the work ourselves on our new build, so I decided to start sharing our journey, thinking others may be interested in what we were doing. I'm a goal setter, so my initial goal was to gain five thousand followers by the time we finished our home.

As one of my presents, he surprised me with a copy of the signed contract and a brick with a key attached to it, symbolizing the home he was going to build for me.

Shortly after our first post, we closed on our loan and began our build. Our general plan was to hire subcontractors for anything we did not know how to do—such as rough plumbing and spray-foam insulation—and then do everything else ourselves. We planned on doing lots of DIYs, sourcing materials from Craigslist, Facebook Marketplace, architectural salvage stores, and back rooms of warehouses. We knew there were projects we would not finish right away but figured that after we earned our certificate of occupancy, we could finish the rest as we were able. It would be a nice home—nothing over-the-top, nothing worthy of a magazine cover—and it would be ours, and we would save so much money doing it ourselves.

Four months after we closed on our loan, our Instagram had grown to twenty thousand followers. We thought it was neat, but we had no idea how it was about to change our lives. Then I received a DM. It was from a new door company based in Florida that wanted to know if we would be willing to let them put doors on our home in exchange for pictures and marketing. Daniel and I were shocked. If this company wanted to work with us, what other companies might also be interested in using our home and platform in exchange for product?

In that moment, our entire thought process changed. My focus then became to grow my platform as much as I possibly could by providing value, knowledge, and inspiration to our followers while at the same time seeking out brands that might be willing to partner with us. It was a painstaking process, but in time, more companies wanted to become a part of our home-building project.

With each deal we closed, our excitement grew. Our goals transformed from building a home pieced together with secondhand materials to something more beautiful than we had ever imagined. Rather than designing our home around the materials we could source, we designed it exactly how we wanted.

We love our home and our exciting journey that has now led to you holding this book. Ours is the story of a couple from Florida who were either brave enough or crazy enough to take a leap of faith and build the home of their dreams, primarily with their own hands, even though they had never built a house before. And we know that this will not be the journey for everyone, so we have taken the lessons we learned, along with the original ideas that drove us to build our home ourselves, and we are going to share with you how you can create your own dream home on a budget.

> Our goals transformed from building a home pieced together with secondhand materials to something more beautiful than we had ever imagined.

Even if you aren't building from the ground up, there is plenty of information and inspiration in this book to help you renovate, remodel, or even just decorate your home for far less than the going

market rate, without having to negotiate brand deals. We'll teach you some best practices for how to do projects yourself, explain where to source materials, offer tricks and tips for planning, and share advice to help you through the process.

As you read through this book, remember that it's not just a one-time read but rather a reference book. It's meant to be used as a guide throughout your home-building or renovating journey that you can come back to again and again whenever needed. Even if you're just dreaming of building someday or are in the beginning stages of planning, you can read through the projects and decide which ones you are capable of tackling, which ones you may need to do a little more research on, or which ones you need to find someone in your life to help you with.

The following pages are packed full of information, checklists, guidelines, recommendations, and tools to help you make decisions, save money, eliminate stress, and make sure the home you create is not only beautiful but built to stand the test of time.

Let's get to it!

Please join us on our journey as we delve into the world of creativity, discovery, and all things DIY as we hope to help and inspire you to begin your own journey.

Sincerely,

Noell and Daniel

Plan for Success

While starting a new project is exciting, and you may want to jump into it headfirst, failing to plan sets you up for failure. In Part One, we share some tips and best practices to help set you up for success.

ONE

MENTAL PREPARATION

I f you are planning on building, renovating, or redecorating your space, it's important to prepare your-self mentally for what you're about to embark on. Undertaking a project of this magnitude is not for the faint of heart. It requires vision, determination, and the willingness to push on when the going gets tough.

We were warned by so many people that building a home together would be a detriment to our marriage. Now that we are on this side of the build, we can understand why they would say that. There are so many decisions to be made, and we sometimes had different opinions. Not to mention, a budget can stretch only so far, and we had differing views on how it should be spent. We each had our non-negotiables, and it took a lot of focus and commitment to work together to ensure we were both happy. The long hours and mental stress exhausted us to our core, making it harder to get along and work together. However, we learned a few things along the way to help minimize this stress.

If you're tackling these projects alone, you might not run into the same issues. But if you're taking them on with another person—be it a spouse, a business partner, a family member, or a friend—first, acknowledge and understand that you each have your own expecta-tions, and be open and honest about them. Make a list of the top five things each of you would like to have in the home and place them in

> Make a list of the top five things each of you would like to have in the home and place them in order of importance.

order of importance. This way, as you work through the budget, you'll have clear priorities in place. Try your best to highlight at least the top three priorities from each list, but go in order of importance and, as much as possible, keep it equal and balanced.

THINGS TO UNDERSTAND BEFORE YOU START

There are a few things you should understand before diving in that we only know *now*, after going through the process:

1. **Understand your reasons for wanting to build or renovate your home.** This will give you clear purpose and drive. When things get tough, you can remind yourself of the reasons you began your journey in the first place. For us, we wanted to be able to create exactly what we wanted, learn and be involved in every aspect of the build, and take the information and skills we learned and implement them in future jobs.

2. **Understand that there will be issues.** No project is seamless. There are some projects that have fewer problems than others, but no matter how well you plan and prepare, something will arise. Know this going in so that when issues do surface, instead of being surprised and getting upset, you can look at each other, laugh, and say, "Hey, at least one of those issues we knew to expect is over." Changing your mindset to look at problems that arise as a natural part of the process, rather than as interruptions and frustrations, will help keep tempers and emotions in check.

3. **Understand that your life will revolve around your home.** Whether it's a full home build from the ground up or a small renovation, the more involved you are in the actual process, the more consumed you will be. Whether DIY-ing it, managing your own subcontractors, or working with a builder, it will add stress to your life. You'll be forced to make snap decisions that you will have to live with for years to come. The pressure to make the right decisions can feel overwhelming. By the way, decision fatigue is a real thing, and you'll absolutely suffer from it during a full home-build process.

By the way, decision fatigue is a real thing.

HOW TO PREPARE

So, knowing that there will be added stress, problems, and issues that come up along the way, along with decision fatigue, what can you do to mentally prepare? Consider the following:

- Research and plan as much as possible in advance. The more prepared you are before you start, the less stressful it will feel when it comes time to make decisions.
- Do your best to find time to relax, have date nights with your spouse, or spend time with friends where you are not allowed to discuss the build. Rather, use this time to enjoy life and dream about the memories you will make in the home you're creating.
- Also, remember that many home projects can be stressful for children. As you find yourself surrounded by tile, wood, and paint samples, you understand that it's all temporary and it's only a short while until life returns to normal, but children don't understand time like we do. They may think you're going to be a stressed-out, overwhelmed person forever. (At one point, one of our daughters told someone her mommy's favorite hobby was picking out tile.) So, take time to reassure them that this will last only a little while, talk to them about how wonderful it will be once your home is completed, and start envisioning with them all the new memories you will create together in your beautiful new home. Let them "help" design their room or spaces they will use or give them "jobs," such as seeing who can build the biggest pile of scrap lumber. (Our kids loved using a magnet pole to see who could collect the most screws from the dirt.) Involve them in the process in any way you safely can.

Note: Throughout the book, when we refer to a *contractor*, this means the *builder.* So, anyone doing their own work is seen as the contractor, though you would never use that term. It would be more like *self-contracting* or *owner-builder.* Because of that, anyone *you* hire would be considered a subcontractor, and it would also be rare for a trade to have a general contractor license.

TWO

LET'S TALK MONEY

Building a home on a budget or doing renovations on a budget can mean so many different things to different people. Whether you're renovating a room for five thousand dollars, building a tiny home for fifty thousand dollars, or working with a much higher budget for a brand-new build or complete home renovation, there are ways you can save money and create your dream home for less. Whatever amount you plan on spending, try your best to have at least an extra 15 to 20 percent available for unexpected expenses.

If you are working with a construction loan, which is a short-term loan to cover only the cost of the home build (and can also include the land you're building on), and do not have a builder, you may be expected to pay out of pocket, and the bank will reimburse you once you pass inspection of different parts of the home. For us, the bank gave us 15 percent at closing to get 25 percent of the work done under a construction loan. This meant we had to pay out of pocket to get the next 10 percent done. Once it was completed, we called for a bank inspection. When they verified the work was done, the bank released the 10 percent of funds to pay us back, but by then we were already working on the next 10 percent using our own money.

> While beautiful things are nice to look at, it's more important to choose things that will make your life easier and save money in the long run.

Maintaining enough cash to keep the build going while also running our company and paying payroll proved to be a serious challenge. If you're going with a construction loan, keep in mind that you will need quite a bit of available cash. Not all loans may be set up this way, so it's smart to ask your loan officer what the payment disbursement schedule looks like. If you happen to be self-employed like we are, finding a loan officer who will advocate for you and work with you to secure financing is very important. Even if you're not thinking of building for a few years, it may be wise to sit down with a loan officer to talk through your situation to see if there are any financial changes you need to make in order to better your chances of getting a loan. In some cases, you'll need to have been doing things a certain way for twelve months for a bank to consider it, so if there is anything you might need to be doing differently, it's better to start earlier than later.

Once you have your loan approved or your cash ready to go—whether for a full home build or a renovation—look at your budget carefully. Make sure to stay as close as possible to the numbers allotted for each category. What happens in many cases is that as each trade comes in, they will try to up-sell you.

And yes, upgraded windows and thicker plywood sound great. But if you go just a little over budget in each category, even a little, you may be forced to skimp by the time you get to the finishes—the products you see every day, like flooring, countertops, cabinetry, and faucets—because you are out of money. You won't see the underlayment under your shingles every day, but you *will* see the beautiful light fixtures. As you make each decision, keep the total budget in mind, and remember that it's important to have as much money as possible left in your budget for finishes.

That said, it's equally vital to think carefully through each decision and to consider function and durability *first* in some cases. While beautiful things are nice to look at, it's more important to choose things that will make your life easier and save money in the long run. For example, having

Types of loans

It would take a whole book to talk about all the ins and outs of the various types of loans available, but we wanted to list some here so you could begin researching to consider what's best for you.

- Construction loan: Short-term loan to cover the cost of building

- Renovation loan: Loan that gets wrapped up with your mortgage based on the home's value *after* renovations

- Cash-out refinance: Replaces your mortgage with a bigger loan and allows you to use any equity you've built up

- Home equity line of credit: Loan that acts like a credit card and allows you to use funds as you need them and repay them at either a fixed or variable interest rate

beautiful cabinetry with poorly made hinges and hardware will end up costing you more sooner rather than later to have them fixed after daily wear and tear.

HOW TO BUILD A BUDGET

Use these guidelines as a framework to get started on creating your building or renovation budget.

Architectural Plans: 1 percent

Permits and Fees: 1 percent

Site Prep: 4 percent

Foundation: 10 percent

Plumbing Rough-In: 5 percent

Framing: 7 percent

Trusses: 6 percent

Roof Sheathing and Felt: 3 percent

Windows: 3 percent

Electrical Rough-In: 2 percent

HVAC: 8 percent

Roofing: 3 percent

Insulation: 2 percent

Siding: 5 percent

Exterior Trim/Soffits: 3 percent

Drywall/Plaster: 6 percent

Exterior Doors: 2 percent

Bathroom Tile: 3 percent

Interior Trim and Doors: 5 percent

Interior Painting: 3 percent

Cabinets and Vanities: 4 percent

Exterior Painting: 1 percent

Plumbing Fixtures (with installation):
   3 percent

Electrical Fixtures (with installation):
   2 percent

Hardware/Mirrors/Shelving/Showers:
   1 percent

Floors: 3 percent

Appliances: 2 percent

Driveway/Walks/Garage Door:
   1 percent

Sewage: 1 percent

THREE

ORGANIZATION AND PLANNING

W e planned for *seven years* before we started our build. That gave us plenty of time to figure out exactly what we wanted and to organize our thoughts and plans. You can organize your ideas electronically using sites like Pinterest or do it manually. A large three-ring binder with dividers or even a filing box may be needed, depending on the size of your project and the level of detail you desire.

Let your imagination run wild. Collect images of anything you find beautiful, interesting, or functional. As you get closer to your build, renovation, or DIY project and walk through the preparation process, you will narrow down these ideas to the things you will *actually* include, selecting from the broad range of options available to you.

You'll also want to create a clear system of organization to store important paperwork and communications regarding your build. The more organized you are, the easier it will be to make decisions, saving you time and money. If any issues arise, you can easily provide documentation or receipts.

We used physical file folders to organize our ideas and paperwork. Here are the categories we created:

> The more organized you are, the easier it will be to make decisions, saving you time and money.

- **Exterior Features:** We collected elements of other exteriors we loved so when it came time to design our home, rather than feeling overwhelmed by our options, we had a general idea of what we both wanted. We collected examples of wraparound porches, rooflines, front doors, and window sizes, to name a few.
- **Interior Design Ideas:** You'll want to organize design ideas for each room in your soon-to-be home. Collect lighting ideas, vanities you love, cabinetry styles, flooring, ceiling ideas, and so on.
- **Priority List:** Remember the priority list of nonnegotiables we previously discussed? This is a great place to start developing a list of the things that are most important to each of you.
- **Correspondence:** This category covers all communication with suppliers, bids from subcontractors, contracts, bank documents, paid invoices, and receipts.
- **Permitting:** Collect printouts of everything required for your city or county and copies of all permits.
- **Important Documents:** Keep track of things like paperwork from the bank, warranties, manuals for appliances, or other items used in construction.

TIMELINE

Knowing the timeline of a build or remodel will help you in your planning process. Knowing at what point you need to have your plumbing fixtures, lighting design plan, and flooring chosen will prevent you from making a snap decision, choosing something you don't truly love, spending additional money by having to make change orders, or costing you time by delaying a part of the project because you weren't ready. This should be a general timeline; if you have a builder and subcontractors, it will move faster than doing it yourself.

Stay in touch with any subcontractors or anyone else involved in the project to see if the schedule changes or evolves as the build progresses.

Also, before your home build, renovation, or project begins, have your engineered plans finalized.

Step 1: Site preparation—two weeks to one month. Before this process begins, you'll need to know where you want your house to sit on your lot and the exact angle you'd like it to face. The timing for this step depends on how heavily wooded your lot is.

Step 2: Footers and foundations—two to four weeks. This varies depending on the type of foundation you go with.

Step 3: Framing—one to two months. You'll need to have all interior walls decided on. If you are uncertain about any room's layout—or door or window placement—stay in close contact with your framer (if not framing yourself). This will save time and money to make these changes before the walls are put in place.

Step 4: Mechanicals (siding, roofing, HVAC, and electrical)—four to eight weeks. You'll need to know your lighting plan, have your plumbing fixtures chosen, know where you want or *don't* want your vent covers located on your walls and ceiling, and have your roofing and siding materials selected.

Step 5: Insulation and drywall—one to two weeks. You'll need to know what type and where you want insulation. If your kids' rooms are upstairs, you may want extra insulation between your floors, or maybe in the walls surrounding your laundry room if those noises bother you, or maybe surrounding the owner's suite for added privacy.

Step 6: Flooring, trim, and paint—one to two months. You will need to have your materials on site by this time, meaning your selections are already made and product has already been ordered well in advance to arrive by this point. As you are researching these products, make sure to take note of delivery times so you ensure they are delivered on time and ready to be installed. These selections include wood or vinyl flooring, tile, architraves, baseboards, crown molding, interior doors, cabinetry, and built-ins.

Step 7: Exterior finishes—two to four weeks. Any brick, stone, or remaining siding selections will need to be on site by this point.

Step 8: Fixtures and appliances—two to four weeks. Light fixtures, faucets, bathtubs, toilets, sinks, shower units, cabinets, countertops, appliances, and any carpeting you chose for your home need to be on site.

Step 9: Driveways, walkways, and exterior doors—one week. At this point, you need to have all your exterior doors on site as the dunnage doors will be coming off and your beautiful selections put into place. You need to know what you will be using for your driveway and walkways and have those materials on site.

Step 10: Cleanup—one week. Don't forget to allow time to clean up construction debris and drywall dust to get your home move-in ready.

Step 11: Landscaping—two to three weeks. To get a better estimate, you will need to know how much landscaping you'll be doing and the size of your lot. Rules and regulations vary from place to place, so check your local codes or loan policy to learn how much sod and if any plants or trees are required.

Step 12: Time to get your certificate of occupancy and start moving in. In any build, getting your certificate is the final major step that shows the county deems your home fit to live in. Different areas have different requirements; for example, you may need to have only one functioning bathroom to obtain your certificate, meaning you could finish your main bathroom, get your certificate, and then finish the kids' bathrooms as you can afford them.

SOURCING MATERIALS

Now that you've done some planning and prepared yourself mentally, it's time to look for the best prices for materials and research like you have never researched before. Just when you think you've called enough suppliers, read enough resources, and talked to every possible person, you are about halfway there. Keep going. Some of the material resources we discovered were found after we thought we had researched as much as we possibly could. If you're like us, you might have more available time than money, so you'll want to uncover every possible resource that can provide materials to help you with your home build or renovation.

One of our biggest money savers came from a conversation with our lumber and window supplier. During our conversation, they mentioned in passing a company called Ready-Frame. They tried to move the conversation forward, but we redirected it to learn more information, and it ended up being a game changer for us. We saved more than $30,000 by using the Ready-Frame system and framing our home ourselves.

The resources you find for materials will vary based on where you live in the country, but some of the vendors we used that are nationwide include BMC, Capitol Lighting, SapienStone, Jeffrey Court, Viewrail, and Empire Moulding & Millwork.

SOURCING MATERIALS FROM NONTRADITIONAL SOURCES

The big-box and national stores aren't the only places to find traditional building materials, such as cabinetry, wood beams, bricks, tiles, appliances, windows, lighting, faucets, or pretty much anything else that goes into a home. You would be amazed at the amount of materials you can source from places like Facebook Marketplace, Craigslist, architectural salvage places, or stores like Habitat for Humanity

ReStore, where builders donate leftover building supplies for a tax credit. By purchasing materials this way, you can save money and keep items from going to landfills as well.

There are a few things to consider:

Make connections. More on this in the next section, but if you can find someone remodeling or dismantling their home, you can sometimes find materials like cabinetry, wood beams, bricks, appliances, or wood flooring. Making connections with contractors can also be helpful because there are always materials left over from jobs, and if they know you're looking for something, they can keep an eye out for you. We have one friend who, with permission from a construction superintendent, collected leftover lumber from each jobsite for *three years* and framed his entire home with it. At the time, the total value of that framing package was over $25,000. Think of how valuable that savings was toward his overall budget.

Think outside the box. Think of ways you can use materials in an unconventional manner to add character and charm to your home. If you stumble upon a supply of bricks, use those as flooring in your laundry room or on your porch. Reclaimed wood is great to put on a ceiling to add visual interest. If you come across a good lighting option, even if it's not exactly what you had in mind, consider painting or reconfiguring it to match your style.

Find the exceptions. Once you've resourced as much as you possibly can from these avenues, it's time to start looking for new materials. Begin by going to your local retailers and asking if they have any returns or discontinued items you could see, or find out when their next sales are. Our local door supplier has an entire warehouse of doors that were returned for various reasons, one being simply the customer changed their mind. Before we partnered with a different door company, we found a gorgeous solid mahogany double door—which was exactly what we wanted—valued at $8,000 retail in their warehouse, and they were going to sell it to us for $1,600. Another friend of ours was able to get every window in their home at a substantial discount from a custom order that had been returned to Lowe's. If you find something like this

Tip: Store any advance-purchased items in a garage or storage pod. If the items are sensitive to the weather or moisture, a climate-controlled storage unit or extra room of your home would work as well. For example, appliances, windows, and tile can be stored in a garage, whereas wood doors, wood flooring, and cabinetry should be stored in a climate-controlled area.

in advance, you can change the specs of your home to match exactly what you find, so start the search for materials early.

Consult the Yellow Pages. There will be materials that you just cannot find discounted, so how do you ensure you're getting the best price? Call *all* the places. When we were pricing out our lumber, we had an entire notebook sheet covered front and back with suppliers to call for this one thing alone. If we thought they might deliver to us, even if they weren't directly in our area, we called them. A few hours spent on the phone can equate to *thousands* of dollars in savings.

Ask questions. Something that may seem like common sense is not necessarily true. For example, what do you think the cheapest would be: a 7-foot door or an 8-foot door? The 7-foot door seems like it would be cheaper because it's smaller, right? But the 8-foot door is actually cheaper because it's a standard size, whereas the 7-foot door is considered a custom order.

MAKING CONNECTIONS

An old adage, "It's not *what* you know, but *who* you know," rings true when trying to build or renovate a home on a budget. Living in a relatively small town like we do, making connections is our favorite way to do business.

Talk with family and friends. See who they may know that they could introduce you to. We're not talking about looking for a handout here but rather making genuine connections and finding ways you can develop mutually beneficial relationships.

Never tell your budget. When you call a random supplier, you have no idea if you can trust what they are saying or if they're offering their best price. For example, we didn't have a roofing connection in the beginning, so we went to a store and asked for a bid. They called us a week later, and the first question they asked was "What was your budget again?" Never answer this question. Make them give you a price. They quoted Daniel a price, and when he reminded them that he was also in the industry, they immediately took $5,000 off. Daniel said, "Thanks, but no thanks," and we took our business elsewhere. When we finally made a connection in the roofing supplies industry, we were able to find the materials for $16,000 less than the previous company had quoted us. You want to make sure you are getting the best price possible, and having a connection in the industry will help ensure that happens.

Barter and trade. Whatever service you offer the world, see if you can find a way to exchange services rather than money. When we put in our paver driveway, a friend allowed us to use his crews at cost, and in exchange we let him use our crews to do his remodel at cost. In addition to making connections to secure the best pricing, if there is something you don't know how to do, you may be able to find someone who would be willing to come help you learn how to do it. Not only could this save you money, you'll learn a valuable skill that you can use in the future. We learned so much this way.

A WORD OF CAUTION

As exciting and amazing as it seems to build your own home, we would be remiss if we did not discuss the importance of following your local building codes and zoning regulations, whether you're building from the ground up or doing a renovation, or maybe even a DIY project that requires you to be mindful of your local codes and regulations. Your local building department can point you in the right direction. You can also speak with a contractor or building inspector to ensure you're meeting—and even exceeding—local codes. We sought out the wisdom of several contractors and developed a good relationship with our county inspector. This allowed us to build a home that our county inspector told us was the best-built house he had seen in over twenty years on the job.

Tip: When we signed our lumber contract, we locked in our price if lumber went higher, but if it went lower, we would pay the lower price. When the day came to order our lumber, we made sure to check lumber prices, and our cost had gone down $5,000. When the lumber company called to collect payment, the total had not changed. So, we reminded them about our contract, and they corrected the total in our favor. This is why it's so important to keep your documents organized and stay on top of things; it could save you lots of money.

PART TWO

Doing the Hard Work to Make It Beautiful

As you scroll through beautiful images on Pinterest or Instagram, it's easy to see the finished product and fantasize about achieving the same end result in your own home. But it's important to remember that a lot of hard work goes into creating the beautiful spaces shown in those images.

FOUR

DIY BASICS

One of the best ways to save money during a home build or renovation is to do things yourself. With the many resources available to us these days, you can learn how to do almost anything online through YouTube videos, tutorials on blog posts, and books on almost every topic you can imagine.

Even if you take on only parts of your project, you can save money by completing portions of your build by yourself. Whether as complicated as framing your own home or as simple as painting your walls—whatever level of time, work, and skill you can pour in—you will see savings and discover the pride and satisfaction in your home that only sweat equity can bring when you choose to DIY.

How do you know exactly which projects are best to do yourself and which to hire out? For each person, this answer will be different. We share with you what we chose to subcontract out and why, plus share our tips for finding quality subcontractors and builders to work with.

It's important to note that the projects we've included throughout don't necessarily offer *exact* steps, as each home is different, and dimensions will vary greatly—not to mention the variety of styles and preferences. We do, however, offer ideas and a framework for each, with steps and tips to help set you up for success as much as possible.

> You will see savings and discover the pride and satisfaction in your home that only sweat equity can bring when you choose to DIY.

CHOOSING SUBCONTRACTORS

As previously mentioned, if you're doing your own work, you are seen as the contractor, and anyone you hire would be considered a subcontractor.

The main things we chose to sub out were our drywall, insulation, roofing, plumbing, and part of our siding. We chose these items for various reasons; namely, the cost to do them ourselves far outweighed the cost to use subcontractors—whether that cost was time or money.

For example, the subcontractor installed and finished the drywall throughout our entire home in three days for only $4,400. It would have taken us several weeks and a lot of stress to hang it ourselves. So, it made much more sense for us to hire it out. The same thinking applied to the spray-foam insulation. For the $15,000 it cost us, there was no way we could even acquire the equipment and supplies at that amount had we tried to do it ourselves.

> We decided the risk was not worth the savings.

Other DIYers may be willing to take on roofing, but because our home was well over 30 feet tall with a $^{10}/_{12}$ pitch, we decided the risk was not worth the savings. We also decided to sub out almost all rough plumbing because we were not as experienced in that area, and while we were willing to learn countless other things, we chose to take this one off our plate.

FINDING QUALITY PEOPLE

For the items you decide to sub out, how do you find quality people to work with you on your home? If you are anything like us, we were putting so much blood, sweat, and tears into our home, making it as perfect as possible, that we didn't want to have anyone step foot on the property whom we did not trust to do their work with excellence.

Here's how to go about finding quality people:

1. Spread the word about what you're looking for. Word of mouth can lead to finding qualified subcontractors or builders.
2. Once you have some names, it's time to do some heavy research. Start with checking to see that they are properly licensed and insured. Interview them to see how your personalities mesh.
3. Always get at least three bids. Remember that the cheapest is not always the best.

4. Ask for references and speak with previous clients they have worked with. Ask those homeowners how they felt about the quality of work they did, if they were responsive, if they were open to feedback, if they kept a clean jobsite, or if they always asked for a payment even when work wasn't completed. And ask if they'd ever hire that contractor again.

5. Once you've narrowed it down to your top choice, visit a jobsite they are currently on. Take notes as to the cleanliness and attitudes you see. Speak with some of their subcontractors or employees and find out if they are paid on time or if they have ever had issues with bad checks. These questions will give you insights into how they run their business; how they treat their homeowners, subcontractors, and employees; and how they manage their finances. Remember to never pay all your money up front, and agree on a clearly defined draw schedule, reserving 10 percent of the payment until all punch list items are complete.

TOOLS WE FOUND HELPFUL

We thought the tools we had on hand from our small business would get us pretty far into our build. While they definitely did come in handy, we ended up purchasing or renting quite a few tools throughout the building process. For everything we had to do, we researched the cost to rent versus the cost to purchase and then did a cost per use analysis. If the tool was something we would be able to use for years to come, we would just purchase it. For example, when you are building, you are required to have a dump trailer on site. There is a fee to rent it and a fee each time they dump it.

Jigsaw

This was going to add up to about $5,000 over the course of our build. For $8,000, we could purchase our own dump trailer. We financed it through our business account so it did not affect our personal cash, and it has paid for itself countless times over in our business.

Here's a list of tools we used, divided into those that are required versus handy but optional. You may get by without the use of some of these, but if your intention is to build from scratch, they will be necessary.

The following tools were used for our projects:

personal protective
  equipment (PPE)
12-inch sliding compound
  miter saw
circular saws
  (corded and battery powered)
table saw
reciprocating saws
  (corded and battery powered)
framing hammers
sledgehammers
rubber mallet
jigsaw *(corded and battery powered)*
plenty of batteries and
  chargers for your battery-
  operated tools
impact drivers
compact drill
hammer drill
spade handle drill
paddle bit
plumb bob
extension cords *(minimum of
  eight, heavy gauge)*
wet saw
slide cutter *(tile)*
4-inch grinder
stud finder
laser level

palm sander
orbital sander
belt sander
trowels *(various-sized notched,
  flat, and margin)*
multi-tool
chalk line
nail punch
tube cutter
paint sprayer
roller poles and frames
paintbrushes
paint roller grid
drop cloths
speed squares
framing square
string line
tape measures
razor knife
X-Acto knife
fondant roller
seam roller
5-gallon buckets
wheelbarrow
shovels
post hole digger
levels *(8 feet, 6 feet, 4 feet,
  2 feet, and torpedo)*
straight edge

Shop-Vac
blower
saw blades
large assortment of bits and
  drill bits
large air compressor with a
  minimum of three long
  hoses
ladder
scaffolding
sandpaper
knee pads
wood glue
wood putty
caulk gun
nail guns
  *(framing nailers; finished
  nailers, every gauge size you
  can think of; siding nailers;
  roofing nailers. We already
  had all of these but found it
  handy to have the battery-
  powered nailers as well. We
  purchased four different
  battery-powered nail guns
  during our build and still use
  them to this day.)*

The following tools are optional
but handy:

jobsite radio for music (keeps up morale)

portable pop-up tent (shade for hot climate areas)

fans or heaters (provide comfort for inclement
    weather)

planer

transit level

chain saw

tractor or skid steer with multiple implements
    (bucket, forks, grapple, and box blade)

hydraulic dump trailer

generator

nail gun

Note: It's important to follow *all* safety instructions as outlined by each tool's manufacturer guidelines and to wear personal protective equipment (PPE) when using them, or when visiting a construction or remodel site. Failing to do so could result in serious injury—and even death. As much as you might want to rush to get something done, it's just not worth it. So, please be careful and wear your safety gear! This could include hard hats, steel-toe or safety boots, protective gloves, hearing protection, full-face shields, safety glasses or goggles, respiratory protection, fall protection, or any specific clothing if your project involves welding or live electricity.

FIVE

DESIGN AND STYLE

————————————·————————————

As important as it is to build your home structurally sound, creating a foundation of beauty will make it easier to decorate, regardless of your personal style. Even on a budget, there are simple things you can do in every room to add dimension, visual interest, and beauty. We joked at one point that there wasn't a single room in our entire house that was simply drywall and paint. While this made it frustrating when we were trying to hurry and finish, we are grateful that we added so many beautiful elements that truly make our home special.

But even without those finishes and collabs, you can still afford designer style in your home. It may take longer to get it where you want it, and it may take more digging and searching to find those prize gems, but we have done it on a dime many times in our own home, so we know that you truly can too.

DISCOVERING YOUR STYLE

Before you begin building or renovating your home, it's important to define your style. It can be easy to fall into the trap of thinking you need something because someone else has it or it's the trendy thing to do. But understanding and defining your personal style and preferences, along with how you plan to use each space, will allow you to focus your search on the things that truly bring *you* joy, and keep you from wasting money on unnecessary items. Then you can decorate and accessorize to your heart's content once you've created some of these foundations.

This is also where sites like Pinterest can come in handy. Begin collecting pictures of architecture, rooms, and styles that you like, then notice: What are the common themes? What elements are you drawn to most?

It's amazing what you can do once you know what you like and what aesthetic you're looking for.

Here are some of the major design and architectural styles. Study each one by searching images on the internet and decide which most match your style. If you're building from the ground up, this will greatly inform some of your major choices. For example, we knew we wanted a modern-style farmhouse, so this eliminated a lot of other styles and items that we might have considered purchasing.

And if you're renovating an existing home with an existing architectural style that's different from what you'd like, look to see which elements you can bring into a room or space. It's amazing what you can do once you know what you like and what aesthetic you're looking for. The list here is not exhaustive, but it will at least get you started on your journey if you don't already have a good understanding of what style you're trying to create.

Adobe: Rustic feel with natural, earthy colors; commonly constructed of clay or mud; wooden beams

Antebellum or Southern: Large pillars, two-story balconies, grand entrances, open stairways

Art Deco: Geometric shapes; velvet, gold, or chrome; black and gold combo; palm trees

Beach or seaside: Similar to coastal, but a little more casual, relaxed, or playful

Bungalow: Typically one story; smaller square footage but open living spaces and large windows to make them feel more spacious; known for their dormers, pitched gable roofs, and covered porches

Cape Cod: Clean lines, simple rectangular shape with minimal ornamentation, clapboard or shingle exteriors, dormer windows, and a large centrally located chimney

Coastal: Whitewashed woods; natural fibers such as seagrass, jute, rattan, and wicker; cool tones reminiscent of the sea, such as blues, greens, and whites; open floor plan; textures found on the seashore, such as sand, shells, or rocks; light-colored floor coverings; lots of natural light

Colonial: Simple and symmetrical

Cottage: Small, modest, and cozy

Craftsman: Shingled siding, stone, open and exposed beams, custom built-ins

Beach or seaside →

Modern Colonial →

Farmhouse: Two-story home with a wraparound porch, often features siding and shutters

French country or provincial: A softer look and feel, symmetrical or balanced proportions, steep roofs, porches with balustrades

Georgian: Classical architecture, symmetrical, large center entryway, often with brick exterior

Industrial: Raw, exposed material; brick; unfinished wood; concrete; metal; leather; browns, grays, black, deep greens, and reds; large open spaces

Log home: Literally constructed of unmilled logs, rustic but cozy

Mediterranean: Stucco exterior, terra-cotta tiles used for both roofing and sometimes flooring, cheerful exterior with natural sunny and earthy tones used within

Mid-century modern: Simple, clean, and minimal pieces crafted from warm woods; practical and durable; warmer color palette including richer colors like oranges, burnt sage, turquoise, and bright yellow

Minimalist: Clean lines, simple shapes, monochromatic palette with color used as only an accent, open floor plans, everything has a purpose

Modern or contemporary: Clean lines; sleek and uncluttered; minimalist; primary hues; modern art; glass, concrete, and steel; abstract forms

Rustic: Natural and raw materials and textiles; reclaimed and unfinished woods, rocks, or stones; exposed beams and brick; burlap; canvas; woven baskets; antlers; jute or animal skin rugs; barn doors; natural color palette including creams, grays, beiges, greens, and muted colors; wood-covered ceilings

Rustic modern: Rustic style combined with clean lines; lots of natural light; cozy textiles, antiques, and mixing some modern furniture with natural materials; bringing the outdoors in through plants, whether real or faux

Scandinavian: Merges architecture with surrounding nature and environment, limited decorative accessories, functional and simple form with clean lines and edges, minimal style that avoids overly detailed touches and curvature, muted tones and pastels; using plants and wood accents to warm up the space

Transitional: Tying together the different styles in a way that represents you and your lifestyle; offers freedom to express individual style, including home additions and renovations, without being locked into one particular design style

Victorian: Heavy, ornate furnishings; opulent, warm, and dramatic

SIX

SOURCING ALL THE THINGS

N ow that you've defined your style, let's talk about where to source the things you'll need to create a home that brings you joy, is filled with beauty, and allows you to live your best life, without breaking the bank by going out and paying retail prices.

SHOP SECONDHAND

Facebook Marketplace, Craigslist, and resell shops on Instagram can be a gold mine for great products. The home improvement industry is booming right now, and people across the country are doing home construction and renovations, which means homeowners are sometimes begging for people to come and take away their old items so they don't have to deal with them.

Don't limit your search to your local area; feel free to search nationwide. After weeks of online hunting, we stumbled across beautiful leaded glass windows for a much lower price than we'd been seeing. They were listed on Facebook Marketplace, and although they were located several hours away in Orlando, Florida, we knew they'd be perfect for our home. So, we loaded up the kids and made the trip down. If you fall in love with a product and can't make the drive, or it's just too far, there may be more ways to work around it.

You can ask the sellers to ship, of course, but if they say they cannot, there are companies like uShip that prioritize making big shipping cost-effective. You simply enter the location where you need something delivered, and people bid on the opportunity to transport it to you. Much like DoorDash or Grubhub, where people make use of their own personal vehicles to deliver meals from restaurants to your home, people sign up to personally deliver your package for a competitive fee. We've done this for several different pieces, including our dresser, the countertop in our kids' bathroom, and more. So don't search only in your area because there may be plenty of great opportunities right outside your town.

ESTATE SALES AND ANTIQUE STORES

People frequently ask where we may have gotten this piece or that, and more often than not, the item came from an estate sale or a garage sale or is an heirloom from someone in our family. Items that came from Noell's grandpa's barn or from her grandmother's home are precious to us, and we've held on to those things because they aren't just beautiful, they also have meaning and history.

The day Noell's grandfather asked her if she wanted to go "pick" his barn, which was a treasure trove of things that had been used in her family for generations, was one of the greatest days of her life. Listening to him share his memories of whom the items belonged to and how he remembered them being used gave them so much value in our eyes. Noell has also flown home from Missouri with her Nanny McCoy's bowls safely tucked among the clothes in her suitcase and has driven seventeen hours with her wrought iron bed strapped to the top of the car. These are the pieces we love the most and that bring us the most joy as we walk through our home, no matter how trendy or stylish they may or may not be.

> You have to know when to wait and when to jump.

Antique stores, flea markets, and estate sales are great places for finding unique pieces you really love—and this goes for building materials too, not just home decor and accessories. Finding items you love from these outlets is a big part of the farmhouse movement, and so many women in the design world love antiques.

If you come across something at an estate sale that you truly love, something so incredibly unique that you've never seen anywhere else, it's probably worth snatching up before someone else does. You can try to negotiate the cost, but even if the seller won't budge on price, don't try waiting until that last day of the sale to come back when everything's half price and when the sellers are just trying to move product and get rid of everything. You have to know when to wait and when to jump.

Essentially, if you are looking for designer style, you'll benefit from adding to your home one-of-a-kind pieces that mix with commercial items. Going beyond box stores for your home decor goes a long way to adding depth and character to your home, and getting those vintage or authentic items secondhand at estate sales, antique stores, and flea markets is a great, affordable way to do it. It may take time, but with the right attitude and patience, you can truly enjoy the hunt. Make sure not to splurge on trendy accessories or decorative accents; they come in and out of style too quickly. However, *do* be willing to invest in pieces you will use the most.

> **Apps and sites to find used items:**
> 5miles
> Buy Nothing Project
> Craigslist
> decluttr
> eBay
> eBid
> Facebook Marketplace
> letgo
> Nextdoor
> OfferUp

LOVE THE SPACE YOU'RE IN

It's also important to be patient with the space you're living in. We know from personal experience how tempting it is to want to hurry and fill up your house straightaway with loads of charm and character representative of the overall style you're going for. Instead, celebrate every new piece that comes into your home. Treasure each new thing that brings you joy without feeling like you must do it all now.

It's better to have a half-empty house that you slowly fill up with things that have meaning than to run out and fill every nook and cranny with items that you don't care about or truly want, which often end up feeling like clutter.

> Think outside the box; don't be afraid to use things in different ways than their intended purposes.

Start with one room at a time, and place them in order of which rooms you spend the most time in. Put your focus and budget toward completing the larger projects before decorating. Think outside the box; don't be afraid to use things in different ways than their intended purposes. An old door can become a gorgeous dining table, for example. Old windows can become a greenhouse wall.

PART THREE

Room-by-Room Guide

Ensuring that the fundamental parts of your home are built properly is so important, but that part of the process is not nearly as fun as making your rooms beautiful. One thing that really impressed the appraiser who appraised our home on two separate occasions was the fact that not a single room in our home had only drywall and paint. Although it was time-consuming to add design elements to every single room—from wall treatments to lighting fixtures—the value and beauty they added to our home made it absolutely worth it and set our home apart from any home the appraiser had set foot in during his entire career.

SEVEN

ALL ABOUT WALLS

T he most basic function of a wall is to seclude us from the elements, but walls actually serve a multitude of purposes. They can bear the weight of flooring systems, trusses, and roofs above them; separate different areas of our homes; and provide privacy. In addition to being functional, they can add dimension and beauty to our homes.

When building or remodeling your home, there are a few questions regarding walls that your builder or architect may ask:

- How tall do you want them? The standard ceiling height is 8 feet. Obviously, the taller the wall, the more your price goes up.
- For a "stick-built" house, otherwise known as a "wooden-framed house," do you want 2×4 or 2×6 exterior walls? The 2×4 walls are more economical, but the 2×6 walls offer more stability as well as additional room for thicker insulation.
- Also, what type of materials would you like to use? Sure, it's all wood, but what type would you prefer? Wood species can have a huge impact on the durability and performance of your home. For example, in our region, framers will typically use spruce for interior walls because it's straighter than yellow pine. For exterior walls, they'll use yellow pine because it's stronger. Another decision will be to use either Oriented Strand Board (OSB) or CDX plywood (which means one side is grade C, the

other is grade D, and X stands for the type of glue used to bind the plywood together) for exterior sheathing or sheeting in order to shave cost from the budget. Plywood is made of many thin layers of wood pressed and held together by strong adhesives. The benefit to CDX is that it's stronger than OSB and is more resistant to water. Additionally, if CDX does get wet, it dries out faster than its counterpart, thus reducing the potential for swelling, mold, and wood rot.

REMOVING WALLS

When remodeling, there's often a concern about removing walls. The two age-old questions when speaking with a remodel client are as follows:

1. Is this a load-bearing wall?
2. If it is, can it still be removed?

Most of the time, even if a wall is "load-bearing," it can still be removed. However, it will require an engineer to approve it as well as give the required method of how to go about it.

WALL TREATMENTS

Once your walls are built and the drywall process completed, it's time to begin making the walls beautiful. Of course, the most basic thing you can do to a wall is paint it, but you can also cover it in wallpaper or add accent wood pieces to turn it into a statement wall.

Note: Peel-and-stick wallpaper is a great option if you are new to wallpaper installation or like to change things up often. It's not nearly as messy as traditional wallpaper; you can remove and reposition it if you mess up the pattern while installing, and it doesn't require many tools to install it. However, as most peel-and-stick wallpaper options are easily removable, the adhesive on this type of wallpaper is not nearly as strong as the paste, making it more likely to peel off the wall on its own, especially in extreme temperatures and humidity.

But what do you do if you're in a farmhouse full of shiplap and you want to create a minimalist or maybe a more mid-century modern aesthetic? Or how do you create the ultimate cozy space when you've just moved into a brand-new industrial high-rise with floor-to-ceiling windows and stainless steel everything?

In our farmhouse entryway, we created a shiplap statement wall (see the "Statement Wall" section in chapter 8). In our living room, we created a mirror wall (see the "Project: Mirror Wall" section in chapter 9). These added a modern touch that worked for our space.

This is a great opportunity to explore more of your foundational style and preferences from chapter 5. Take a look online and find options that match your style. When you can't change the foundational structures, changing wall treatments is one of the least expensive ways to completely transform the look and feel of a room.

PAINT

If you're a DIYer by nature, you've most likely done your fair share of painting, as it's an easy, quick, and inexpensive way to make a huge difference in home decor. However, if you haven't painted a new-construction home before, it's quite different

Ideas for wall treatments:

Paint

Wallpaper

Wallpaper panels

Wainscotting

Crown molding and
   baseboards

Board-and-batten

Shiplap

Brick or stone

Tile

Upholstery

Fabric or tapestries

Curtains

Copper sheeting

Large screens or trellises

Murals

Mirror wall

Painted chalkboard wall

Built-in bookshelves or
   cabinetry

from painting an existing one. The main difference lies in the prep work. Existing homes have all the caulking, drywall patching, and primer coats already done. When painting an existing home, you typically have minimal patching and maybe a little taping before painting. With new construction, you'll have your work cut out for you to accomplish these steps.

On the exterior, the work mainly consists of caulking. Depending on the type of siding you choose, the amount of caulking necessary could greatly vary. For instance, a stucco home will require little caulking compared to a Hardie lap siding home.

On the interior, the main difference is the drywall. If the walls are already painted, it's easy to see

Painting is a lot of fun and can be therapeutic. So turn up your music, and enjoy the simplicity of the work.

any imperfections in the drywall, making it simple to remedy them. In a new-construction home, you don't have this luxury. Your newly installed drywall may need additional sanding and mud work to ensure it's as smooth as possible.

Having a good drywall finisher is imperative. If your finisher is good, during the final stages of their job they'll use lights that cast shadows on the wall to identify and eliminate any imperfections. Without the use of lights, it's difficult to see these imperfections. Before you begin painting, it's a good idea to inspect the walls after the finishers have completed their work. It's also a good idea to hold 10 percent of their final payment until the first coat of primer is applied. This way, if there is any additional finishing necessary, they are motivated to come back for touch-ups.

In new construction, it seems like the painter's job is never done. There are always touch-ups here and

there, places where other workers caused damage or put their dirty hands on finished walls. It's best to do your final punch-out items once all subcontractors are done. This will save you from spinning your wheels. Painting is a lot of fun and can be therapeutic. So turn up your music, and enjoy the simplicity of the work.

CHOOSING PAINT COLORS

To determine which paint colors you want, choose two to three options of each of the colors you like and pick up paint samples for them. Look closely at these paint samples in the sunlight; ideally stand in the room where you're planning on using the color to see which undertones pull or show up in that particular room. If you already have fabric samples for your furnishings, hold the paint samples next to them in the natural light to see if they work well together. Once you think you have the perfect color, purchase a small sample, and paint a section of your wall to make sure you truly love it before you purchase gallons of it. If you're looking for the perfect interior white, remember that stark whites will clash with most decor. Going with something like Sherwin-Williams Alabaster will provide the perfect white that will go with everything.

In addition to basic wall color, paint is an inexpensive way to add character and visual interest to your home. You can try painting vertical or horizontal stripes, two tones with one color on top and another color on bottom, or geometric shapes created with tape (including mountain walls), scallop borders, and rainbows or clouds in a child's room. You could use simple paint strokes in a favorite color palette, sponges cut into a shape that matches your theme, words, chalk walls—the ideas are endless.

> Guide to choosing paint sheen:
> Living room: satin or eggshell
> Bathroom: semigloss
> Kitchen: semigloss
> Adult bedroom: flat, matte, or
>   eggshell
> Kid's bedroom: satin or semigloss
> Trim: semigloss

PAINTING

Paint plays such an integral part of your home. The exterior color you choose is the first thing people notice when they arrive at your home. The interior color on your walls sets the tone for every room in your home and is statistically proven to affect your mood. Paint colors are the base that help tie in accents, cabinetry, and statement walls. And depending on the style you're going for, this ties in directly to the colors and palettes that you'll want to bring to your home, inside and out.

Materials and tools needed:

primer
paint
professional paint sprayer
drop cloths
tape
plastic
paintbrushes
paint buckets
paint strainers
paint rollers and covers
ladders (if painting beyond
   your reach)
caulk guns
caulk
wood putty or filler

Helpful steps for most painting projects:

1. After your inspections, it's time to prep for paint. The drywall finishers create a lot of dust when sanding the walls and ceilings. A paint sprayer is a necessity for the initial part of the paint job, so when spraying the first coat of primer, that dust tends to become airborne and eventually settles in the paint, creating a rough sandpaper-like texture to the walls. A buildup of dust on the walls or ceiling can also cause paint not to stick. It's best to sweep or dust these areas and then vacuum the floors to ensure this doesn't happen, and then lay down drop cloths.

2. Next, tape and cover all the windows and doors with plastic. Overspray is not easy or fun to clean up, so cover all areas you don't want painted. Be sure to suit up with full personal protective equipment before painting, as you will be spraying overhead as well as in confined areas. One tip is to have your primer tinted to 25–50 percent of the main base color to assist with coverage. You'll be surprised at how quickly and easily the spraying goes. For an average-size home, you can prime both interior and exterior in just a couple of short days.

3. Now that you're fully prepped, the painting begins. For the exterior, we recommend sticking with the paint sprayer coupled with back-rolling for the topcoats of paint. You can always roll or brush

window and door trim once the main body is completed, but spraying will be a great time-saver. On the interior, however, we recommend switching to a paint roller and brushes, mainly because there will be a lot of finished items that will be installed after your primer coat, such as cabinetry and flooring. You can't afford to get overspray on these, and the need for finer detail is greater.

4. After the main finishes are installed, in comes the need for finished carpentry, such as door and window trim, stair railings, and built-ins. This work, once finished, will require a considerable amount of detailed caulking or filler and painting. It can be slow and tedious, but it's important not to rush the process. Take your time making sure that your lines are clean and straight.

5. Although the skill level is much greater and will require a lot of preparation, some people choose to paint trim with a high-volume low-pressure sprayer. We prefer a straight 3-inch paintbrush, so find one that works for you. Some prefer to use painter's tape, but we prefer to paint without it. If you're new to painting or have a less-steady hand, use tape as needed. For freehanding, remember that it's easier to cut the wall paint into the trim rather than cut the trim paint into the wall. So, paint your final coat on trim before finishing the walls.

Project:

PEEL-AND-STICK WALLPAPER

You can source wallpaper across the budget spectrum. One company we really love is WunderWall Mural. We used their wallpaper in our daughter Amelia's room and were so happy with it. It's a peel-and-stick wallpaper, and they have a licensing deal with Shutterstock so they can print literally any design you find on their site. The paper is heavy duty, so even though the first piece ended up crumpled in a ball on the floor (with Noell's tears of frustration pouring over it), once she finally got the hang of it, every crease smoothed out perfectly. If you don't want to wallpaper an entire room, you can create a statement wall, cover half a wall, or even hang a smaller mural like we did in our daughter Ava's room.

Materials and tools needed:

spackle
sandpaper
wallpaper
pencil
level
straight edge
tape measure
X-Acto knife
drywall knife
scissors
squeegee
plastic scraper

Tip: Check the manufacturer's instructions to see how long you should wait after painting your walls before adding wallpaper. Most say two to four weeks to prevent damaging or peeling paint.

Helpful steps for installing wallpaper:

1. Begin by inspecting your wall for any imperfections, rough areas, or holes. Use spackle to fill any imperfections or holes, let dry, then use sandpaper to smooth. Use sandpaper on any other rough areas.

2. Clean the wall to remove any drywall dust, dirt, or pet hair.

3. Remove all light switch and electrical outlet covers, switching off the breakers to be safe.

4. Next, lay out your room. Roll out the paper along the wall. Make a pencil mark on the wall where the roll ends, then slide the paper to that mark, and repeat this process all the way around the room. This allows you to know where all your seams will fall. If one piece of wallpaper is going to be very small, adjust your seams so your pieces are more equal in size.

5. Start from a straight line. Remember that no surface or material is guaranteed to be perfect. Before you begin installing your wallpaper, use either a level and pencil or a laser line to create a plumb line approximately 1/4 inch past where your first panel will end. Then use a level on your ceiling to see how plumb it is. This will tell you how far past your ceiling you'll need to run your paper.

6. Know where to start and finish. The last seam of a repeatable pattern is not going to line up perfectly. Beginning your install in the corner closest to the main door will allow the last seam to be out of the main line of sight. Additionally, if you're using a paper that has a repeatable pattern, your final pattern won't line up. Try to hide this seam in an inconspicuous place.

7. Measure the height of your wall with a tape measure and cut the wallpaper 2–3 inches longer than your desired length to give you some room to make adjustments. Once installed, simply trim off the excess along the ceiling or baseboard using a straight edge and X-Acto knife for a perfect fit.

8. Measure and cut the strips.

9. Lay wallpaper over light switches and outlets. Feel for the four corners, and score an X between them. Cut down the four resulting triangles, neatly tucking any excess paper behind the socket for a smooth finish.

10. Fold paper into thirds, so you can work with a third at a time. Start by peeling back a small section of the backer, about 6 inches, then apply that to the corner. Take your time, and make sure you start off with it correctly positioned.

11. Work your way around the room until you get to doors, windows, switch plates, and so on. To trim the paper as close to the edge as possible, use scissors to make a relief cut before trimming the paper with your X-Acto knife. Use a drywall knife to ensure a straight cut.

12. Run a squeegee over the paper to eliminate any air bubbles and ensure it's properly adhered.

13. Work in small sections until you get the hang of it. Use a plastic scraper and begin pushing down the wallpaper with one hand while you peel back the protective backer with the other. Create a 90-degree angle, and push tightly into that angle with the scraper as you peel the backer with your other hand. Only peel back the protective backer as you push down with the scraper; if you peel away more backer, the paper can stick to itself, creating a major issue (and yes, we speak from experience).

PASTE WALLPAPER

Traditional paste wallpaper requires more patience, planning, and tools but is the better option if you want a quality product that will last. While the paste can be messy, it allows the paper to be manipulated once applied to the wall so you can easily line up edges and seams without having to peel it off and reapply like you would with a peel-and-stick wallpaper. The paste is a stronger adhesive, making traditional wallpaper a better choice for rooms like laundry rooms or bathrooms.

Materials and tools needed:

wallpaper
painter's tape
drop cloths to protect floor
sizing or primer
paint roller
2-inch paintbrush
adhesive (paste)
paint roller tray
clean damp cloth
squeegee
straight edge
X-Acto knife

Helpful steps for hanging paste wallpaper:

1. Once you've selected your wallpaper, decide if you should coat your walls in oil or acrylic primer, or in sizing. Oil-based primer should be used on basic painted drywall, which is most common in current new construction. Acrylic primer is used to lay wallpaper over existing wallcoverings, and sizing is used over plaster walls. This process ensures your paper will adhere properly but also makes it easier to remove if you ever change your mind in the future.

2. Apply painter's tape to any trim around the room to protect it.

3. Lay drop cloths on the floor or over anything you'd like to protect.

4. Follow the general guidelines from "Project: Wallpaper" to get the correct pieces of wallpaper and to align them properly.

5. Now lay them out on a protected surface so wallpaper paste doesn't get on anything it shouldn't.

6. Begin applying primer or sizing to the walls using a paint roller to cover larger areas and a paintbrush to cover the smaller ones. Let dry for a minimum of two hours before proceeding.

7. Pour clear adhesive into a paint roller tray with a $3/4$-inch nap.

8. Using a paint roller, liberally apply adhesive paste to the wall; plenty of paste will help ensure your wallpaper doesn't lift once dry. Applying the paste a couple of inches wider than your wallpaper strip will make it easier to apply your second piece.

9. Use a paintbrush to apply paste close to the ceiling, baseboards, and sockets.

10. As you begin applying the first pieces of paper to the paste-covered wall, work from the top down. Secure the paper across the top, then push it down and over, ensuring it stays along the plumb line. Once you are certain the paper is in the correct position, brush down with the smoothing brush, working from the center out to the edges.

11. Use a squeegee to remove air bubbles, working from the center out.

12. Cut the excess paper at the top and bottom using a straight edge and an X-Acto knife.

13. For the next piece, again, liberally roll paste onto the wall with a paint roller.

14. Check to see where the new piece matches the first piece, then, beginning at the top again, start installing the second piece, making sure it is lined up perfectly as you go.

15. As you reach the bottom, check back to ensure the pattern matches and no gaps exist. If you see it doesn't line up, simply pull it off the wall, line it up correctly, and brush it back into place.

16. To wrap an internal corner, begin by applying paste into and just past the corner. Match up wallpaper patterns and begin brushing it into the corner.

17. When the paper overlaps, you can just leave it to dry. For a professional look, use a fresh blade on your X-Acto knife to cut the papers where they overlap. Remove the excess from the top paper then peel it back to remove the excess of the bottom paper. Push the top paper back into place, and it should line up perfectly.

Project:

WAINSCOTTING

An inexpensive way to add character to any room is wainscotting, though we especially love it in children's rooms. There are countless ways to make it unique and custom to your home, including many different patterns and materials you can use to create the look you want.

Materials and tools needed:

tape measure
boards
4-foot level
pencil
chalk line
table saw
miter saw
18-gauge nail gun
laser level (optional)
stud finder
spackle, wood filler, or joint
    compound
paintable caulk for moldings
    and caulk gun
sandpaper and palm sander

Tip: You can carry your wainscotting to various heights. Our favorite is to carry it three-fourths up the wall on a 9-foot wall, but you can carry it as high or low as you would like. The higher your ceilings, the higher you can carry it.

Helpful steps for installing wainscotting:

1. Decide the look you're going for. You can use beadboard, board-and-batten, or chair railing—there are so many options to choose from.

2. Begin by measuring your space and planning out your materials. To re-create the look we did in Amelia's room, you'll need a top rail and ledge, battens, and if you can't run it directly into your baseboards because of their thickness, a 1×2 added about 2 inches above the baseboard like we did will give your battens something to evenly match up to.

3. As you lay out your pattern, try to avoid placing boards over outlets or switches as this will make the install much easier. Use a level and a pencil to draw a line exactly where your boards will go. You can also mark on either side and use a chalk line.

4. Use a stud finder to locate where to attach boards.

5. Use a table saw and miter saw (where necessary) to cut the pieces to size.

6. Begin installing the boards on these lines, using a nail gun to attach them. Make sure to measure accurately before you cut, and use a level to make sure every board is perfectly plumb before nailing it in.

7. Once all boards are installed, caulk all the seams, fill all the nail holes, let dry, then rub with sandpaper to smooth down. You are now ready for paint, if choosing to do so.

EIGHT

ENTRYWAY AND HALLWAYS

As you open the doors to your home, the first area to greet you is your entryway. How you design and decorate it sets the tone for your entire living space. While making it beautiful is important, thinking through how this space will be used will help make it functional as well. Do you need shoe storage, a place for people to sit and take off their shoes, or a place to store keys or sunglasses? How will your family use this space? What kind of message do you want to send to visitors?

STATEMENT WALL

There are so many options to create an inexpensive yet welcoming space as you enter your home. You could do vertical shiplap, board-and-batten, wainscotting, or simply paint geometric patterns.

In our home, we chose to add horizontal shiplap in our entryway and carried it up our stairwell, instead of having a giant, flat wall. See chapter 7, "All About Walls," for additional ideas and inspiration, and see "Project: Shiplap Wall" later in this chapter for how to install shiplap.

SEATING

Use the entryway to your home, or even to other rooms, as an opportunity to think outside of the box and get creative. Rather than a simple chair, think of unique items that serve as seating options for your entryway. We have antique theater seats in our foyer, but you could also use a pew, wooden storage crates, stools that neatly store under your entry table, or a small bench, or you could even use a built-in that doubles as a place to store shoes, rain jackets, umbrellas, purses, and the like.

STORAGE

If you have an entry table, you can get creative with storage for things like keys and sunglasses. Add a unique bowl or basket, an old crock, a vintage scale that has a place to set things in—anything you can think of and that you love. For storing shoes, add things like larger baskets, large crocks, or wooden bins.

CEILING DESIGN

Though ceilings are often overlooked when designing a space, a beautiful ceiling design can add so much character to a room. Additionally, utilizing the ceiling in your design process draws eyes upward as people enter the room, making the space feel bigger. Try something elaborate like a vault with large wooden beams or simply use a contrasting shade of paint. Or perhaps paint a patterned design on the ceiling to act as a backdrop to gorgeous lighting, creating more of a focal point and allowing the light to really stand out versus getting lost against a vast space.

HALLWAYS

Rather than hallways being long, boring spaces, add design elements to elevate them and add beauty to your home. Here are some of our favorite tips:

- Install horizontally oriented objects such as a chair railing or mirrors.
- Add accent lighting either on the walls or down the length of the room on the ceiling.
- Add texture, such as wallpaper.
- Use this wall space to feature a gallery wall. Either have many pictures in multiple frames, or install a large, oversized frame by using wide molding with mitered corners to serve as a container for smaller pictures and art, creating a statement piece or focal point.

ENTRYWAY STATEMENT CEILING

By the time we realized we wanted to add something visually interesting to our foyer, it was too late to add anything like tray ceilings or beams, or to vault it, or to do most of the other things we found that made foyers beautiful. After some major brainstorming, we came up with a concept we both loved that you can add to any existing flat ceiling. This was actually a simple DIY that creates such a statement when you first walk into our home.

Materials and tools needed:

tape measure
straight edge
pencil
1×2s
18-gauge nail gun
sliding compound miter saw
4.625-inch-by-12-feet primed
    crown molding
1×4s
reclaimed wood or shiplap
1.375-inch-by-8-inch primed
    MDF half-round molding
caulk
primer
paint

Helpful steps for building a statement ceiling:

1. Determine how large you want your statement piece to be and measure it out so it's in the center of the space.
2. With a straight edge, outline in pencil where the new entryway ceiling will go.
3. Cut 1×2s in your desired size of rectangle, nailing it to your ceiling as an outline or guide.
4. Using a miter saw, cut the crown molding at a 45-degree angle so the pieces will fit together perfectly to match the length and width of this rectangle, and nail it into the edge of the 1×2s, leaving a 1-inch reveal.
5. Nail 1×4s into the opposite side of the cove, creating a frame of sorts. Take more 1×2s and flip them on their edge. Nail them into the 1×4s, leaving a 1-inch reveal.
6. Nail 1×4s vertically and evenly spaced across the ceiling on the inside of your box to provide a brace for the reclaimed wood.
7. Cut the reclaimed wood or shiplap to the width of your box, and then begin nailing it into place.
8. If you plan on placing a lighting fixture in yours like we did ours, you will need to purchase longer screws to tie your light fixture into the existing electrical box.
9. Finish the frame with the half-round corner molding, cut to size.
10. Touch up any gaps with caulk, then prime and paint.

SHIPLAP WALL

In our home, we chose to add some modern farmhouse charm by adding horizontal shiplap in our entry-way on what would have otherwise been a giant, flat wall. This added a little depth and dimension without creating too much busyness.

Materials and tools needed:

stud finder
4-foot level
pencil
shiplap
finish nailer
miter saw
a nickel coin
jigsaw
caulk and caulk gun
putty
paint
screwdriver (optional)
two washers (optional)

Tip: We used rough-sawn boards from the Rustic Collection, but you can also cut plywood down or have it cut to your desired widths, generally 5–6 inches wide, at your local home improvement store.

Helpful steps for installing a shiplap wall:

1. Remove any outlet and switch plate covers.
2. Use a stud finder to locate studs and mark them using a pencil and a 4-foot level.
3. Decide on your pattern, making sure your seams land on studs and that no two seams line up on top of each other, to avoid repeating a pattern.
4. Use a miter saw to cut the boards to your desired lengths. You can run your cuts along the edge of the wall, or you can install one piece of shiplap vertically on each edge to give your shiplap something to run into, giving it a more even appearance.
5. Begin installing from the bottom and work your way up. Use a level to ensure your board is level before you nail it in place with your finish nailer. Use the nickel as your spacer between each run.
6. When you approach an outlet or switch plate, draw the outline of the space onto your board, then cut it out using a jigsaw.
7. After all your boards are installed, caulk, putty, and paint.
8. To replace your outlet and switch plate covers, flip the breaker to those outlets and switches, then use a screwdriver to remove the outlet from the box. Now place a couple of washers underneath the small bolt, then reattach the outlet. This will allow your outlets to be even with your wall and outlet covers.

NINE

LIVING ROOM

When designing your living room, it's important to decide whether you want a more formal or casual living space. Some people like to keep their main living area more formal, always looking pristine and ready to entertain, while others, including our family, use it as a space to lay back and enjoy life. You'll need to know how you want your living room to function so you can properly design your floor plan and layout.

Do you envision your living room being used as a family-friendly space where kids and adults alike feel comfortable, or do you envision a more structured space where only adults spend most of their time? Do you want a television in your living room? A large stone fireplace? Beautiful white couches that are not pet- or child-friendly? Knowing how you want this space to function will help you design it.

FROM FUNCTION TO FLOW

Once you know your function, you'll need to determine your flow. First, consider the external flow. Where you place your living room in your home design will be important in determining how your space is used. If you want a casual, open space where everyone can kick back, place your living room in the center of your home, right in the middle of your kitchen and dining spaces. If a more formal, structured space is what you're after, create more defined, separate spaces. Consider the location of the powder room as well; you'll want to make sure it's close enough so that it's easily found but strategically placed to offer privacy.

You'll also need to consider the internal flow, what your focal points will be, how you will center your living around them, and where you will place your furnishings. Make sure to carefully consider the types of furniture you'll place in the room and then design the room to the appropriate size so every piece will fit properly. If you want a large sectional sofa, but your room isn't the right size, you'll end up blocking walkways. Also, make sure to think about things like where you'll place your Christmas tree.

LIVING ROOM LIGHTING

When laying out your floor plan, you must consider lighting—both natural and artificial. You'll want to lay out your living room in a manner that takes the most advantage of natural light. You must also consider the direction of the exposure of that natural light, as which direction it faces will affect how your paint colors will look and what time of day you'll receive the most light.

Once you've determined how the natural lighting will affect your living room, it's time to consider your lighting plan. You can add bold or unique lighting fixtures to create and set the tone for the room. (See more on lighting in chapter 19.) Since your living room will be used for so many varied activities, from cozying up with a book and a cup of hot tea to entertaining your family on holidays, it's very important to remember to include the different types of lighting here. Of course, your statement lighting is what will add the most beauty to your living room, but adding in task lighting and accent lighting is what will allow you to create the ambience that will make your living room feel comforting and cozy.

CREATING COZINESS

Fireplaces add instant warmth and coziness. If you are installing a fireplace and live where you can burn wood throughout the year, that is amazing. If, like us, you live in a warmer climate, installing a direct fireplace vent will give you the ambience of a fire without the heat and fumes.

If you don't have a fireplace built into your home, you could add an electric unit or create the same feeling by adding a faux fireplace that you can fill with candles, logs wrapped in Christmas lights, or electric logs. Or consider finding a reclaimed mantle and filling the fireplace area with books. You can also purchase a premade fireplace from numerous retailers, or even build one yourself.

MAKE A STATEMENT

Though fireplaces often create a natural focal point for a living room, they're not for everyone. Instead, you could make a statement wall, pulling from some of the other sections in this book (see chapter 5 for discovering your style, chapter 7, "All About Walls," or chapter 8 to learn how to install your own shiplap wall).

Here are some of our favorites that would be perfect for a living room statement wall:

- **Bricks:** We created a brick wall in our bedroom (see chapter 13), but it also makes a perfect statement wall for a living room.
- **Shiplap:** From bedrooms to living rooms, shiplap really cozies up a space.
- **Paint:** Use a bold, contrasting color on one wall for an inexpensive, fast, and easy way to dramatically change the feeling of your living room.
- **Large mirrors:** If you've ever priced out a large mirror, you were probably as shocked as we were at the sticker price. If you want to create something that will cover a large, empty wall or reflect light to make your space appear larger, you can build a large mirror wall for less than fifty dollars. This can be made as large or as small as you want.

MIRROR WALL

Large, oversized mirrors are expensive and can easily send DIYers way over budget, but this mirror wall project costs a fraction of the price. Use square, round, or diamond shapes on walls or doors, wherever you'd like to brighten a room and also help a space feel larger.

Materials and tools needed:

small mirrors (8 inches wide by 10 inches tall) from a dollar store or someplace similar
1×4s and 1×2s for frame
miter saw
foam board
box cutter
Gorilla Glue
nails or screws (optional)

Tip: The mirror wall we created was much more rustic than this modern style shown here and fit our farmhouse aesthetic. For ours, we used 1×4s on the outer frame and 1×2s for our interior panes to create a piece that matched our style.

Helpful steps for building a mirror wall:

1. If the mirrors you purchased came in frames, remove them.

2. Determine what size you want your overall mirror to be and use a miter saw to cut your 1×4s to the length and width you want your overall frame and your 1×2s to the appropriate sizes for your panes. While the horizontal boards will need to be cut to the size of each pane, your vertical boards can be the full length of the interior of the project.

3. Arrange the mirrors into the shape and size you want them, leaving gaps between each mirror that match your desired "pane" size.

4. Cut the foam board using a box cutter, and arrange it to match this shape, leaving extra foam board to the side that is the size of the frame you want to use.

5. Use Gorilla Glue to attach the mirrors to the foam board and let it completely dry.

6. Flip the project over and begin assembling your frame. Start by gluing on the four boards that will make up the outer frame. Then nail or screw these together for added stability. The edges can line up squared, or if you want to get extra fancy, you can miter them.

7. Now add interior panes, if you like. Run vertical pieces first, then fit each horizontal piece into place.

8. The bigger you make this entire piece, the heavier it will be, so make sure to securely attach it to the wall.

TEN

DINING AREA

Let's be honest: The dining room is all about the table and the people who gather around it. Some of our favorite life memories are of sitting around old tables with discolored leaves and mismatched chairs, sharing delicious homemade meals and playing card games late into the night with family and friends.

The feelings and memories you create are far more important than worrying about having the latest styles and decor. However, it's still enjoyable to craft a dining area that evokes conversation and brings you joy.

We could go on for a whole chapter on furnishings, accessories, and creating beautiful tablescapes alone. We'll offer some basic dining room foundations but first wanted to mention that there is no need to go out and buy an expensive, fully matching dining room set. Don't be afraid to mix and match materials and textures to create interest. You could either build your own dining room table or find a used one that has the shape and size you need. Then, either buy or find chairs or benches to coordinate.

CHOOSING FURNISHINGS

Generally, it's best to choose a dining room table shape that matches the dining space. However, going with a round or oval table is perfect if you need more room for traffic flow. Round tables are also more

Don't be afraid to mix and match materials and textures to create interest.

conducive to group conversations, whereas rectangular tables promote more intimate conversations between fewer people.

To determine the size your dining room table should be, measure the length and width of your dining area. Subtract 6 feet from the length and width to allow room to move around. Convert to inches to determine the maximum length and width of the dining room table you should get. To determine the size of the rug for your dining room, measure the size of the space that would allow all legs from your chairs to rest on the rug when they are pulled out completely.

DINING AREA ESSENTIALS

Now that we've discussed the obvious, let's look at what makes a great dining room before the table and chairs arrive. If you're building new construction, you'll want to consider the following:

- How many people are sitting down to dinner at your table on a daily basis?
- Do you like to entertain?
- If so, ideally, how many people would you like to have seating for?
- Are you wanting to promote intimate conversations or involve everyone for a group conversation?
- Think about the holidays or special occasions: Do you like to do a formal, sit-down dinner, or is your family more of a "walk through the buffet and find a place to sit in the house" type of family?
- Do you need an area to serve food from or a space to store your fine china and seasonal dishes?

As you think over the answers to these questions, you will gain a better understanding of the type of dining room you will want.

We knew we didn't want to use any of our precious square footage on a formal dining room that we might use only a few times a year. Instead, we opted for a dining space right off the kitchen that served as both a breakfast nook and seating for regular family meals. Because we had another separate dining area on our screened-in porch, we knew we could entertain another family and have plenty of table seating.

For our holidays, we both have large families and would require a table that seated fifty people at minimum to host a sit-down dinner. Adding that kind of seating was not an option for our space and budget, so we focused on the day-to-day and weekly entertaining needs of our family.

Think about the location of your dining area. Keeping it close to the kitchen to make food service as simple as possible will make your life easier when carrying hot pans, but if you have an area of your home where you could place a lot of windows so you and your guests could enjoy the views of nature while dining, that may be more appealing to you.

We discuss lighting design later in chapter 19, but dining room lighting requires some special consideration. As lighting can greatly affect the mood of a room, and this is a place where you'll be spending close, quality time with others, keep in mind as you shop and plan just how important it is to have proper lighting in your dining room. Avoid downlights (lights that literally point down) as much as possible, opting instead for low-hung chandeliers and eye-level lighting. This disperses the light much better and elevates the mood in the room.

If possible, designate a wall or space off your dining area to serve as a wet bar to make it easier to serve drinks. This could be fancy and include items such as an ice maker, beverage center, small sink, and plenty of storage, or it could be as simple as some floating shelves to store your glasses and stemware and a simple countertop underneath. (See the DIY project at the end of this chapter for how to make your own floating shelves.)

DINING ROOM REMODEL

If you're remodeling or renovating, you might be limited in what you can do as far as dining room placement, traffic flow, and natural lighting. We've found that the following elements can be easy ways to create a dining space you love:

- Utilize large mirrors to make your space feel more open.
- Install banquette seating, ideally tucked into a corner. It provides lots of extra seating without taking up much space. You get bonus points if you can find or build a diamond-shaped table to slide into the corner.
- Place a large table in your kitchen that can double as both an island and a dining room table.
- Opt for a round table to give additional seating without limiting traffic flow.
- Incorporate greenery and candlesticks to give it a cozy, inviting feel.
- Use a light and airy color palette with natural decor accents.
- Find a table with removable leaves that can be removed for day-to-day living and installed for entertaining.
- Incorporate design elements that promote conversation among your guests.

Also, don't be afraid to repurpose your dining room for another use that suits your lifestyle and needs. Consider turning your formal dining room into a library or reading room, or maybe a home office. Make it into a guest room by adding sliding barn doors or French doors for privacy. Turn this room into a music conservatory or studio, a bar and game room, a nursery or playroom for little ones, and so on. It's okay to think outside the box.

FLOATING SHELVES

DIY floating shelves are an inexpensive, easy way to add storage, function, and beauty to a room. They are adaptable to any space, as you can make them as long or short and as deep or narrow as you would like—or as space allows—and you can add just one shelf or fill up a whole wall with them. Floating shelves consist basically of two parts: a frame or set of brackets that connect to the wall, and a hollow box that slides over the frame. You can find and purchase brackets premade or DIY the frame as this tutorial teaches.

Materials and tools needed:

wood for shelving
miter saw
drill
wood glue
1$\frac{1}{4}$-inch wood screws
2$\frac{1}{2}$-inch wood screws
stud finder
tape measure
pencil
level
$\frac{3}{8}$-inch dowel rods
multi-tool
orbital sander
wood putty
paint or stain and supplies,
   optional

Tip: To make shelves like ours, use the following:
(2) 1×10×36
(1) 1×2×36
(2) 1×2×6$\frac{1}{2}$
(1) 2×2×34$\frac{1}{2}$
(3) 2×2×6

Helpful steps for building floating shelves:

1. Use a miter saw to trim any wooden boards to fit.
2. Begin by laying out the 1×2×36 and place one 1×2×6$\frac{1}{2}$ on each end, then drill a pilot hole from the longer piece into the shorter one on each end. Apply wood glue on the end of each 6$\frac{1}{2}$-inch piece with the pilot holes.
3. Drill 1$\frac{1}{4}$-inch screws through your pilot holes, driving it from your longer 1×2 into the shorter one.
4. Place a 1×10 board on each side of your assembled 1×2, and drill two pilot holes through them on each end and side.
5. Remove your 1×10 boards, then apply wood glue on one side of the 1×2 frame. Place one 1×10 board on the glue-covered edge, then flip the frame over and repeat the process on the other side.
6. Drill 1$\frac{1}{4}$-inch wood screws through the pilot holes to securely hold the pieces in place.
7. Prepare the frame for assembly by laying three 2×2×6 pieces against the 2×2×34$\frac{1}{2}$, one on each end and one in the middle. Drill pilot holes through the larger piece and into the top of the smaller pieces.
8. Separate, then apply glue to the end with the predrilled hole of each smaller piece. Place back against the longer 2×2 and drill into place using the 2$\frac{1}{2}$-inch wood screws.

9. Use a stud finder to locate the wall studs. If there are no studs where you want to hang the shelf, use drywall anchors for extra support. Mark where you want to hang the frame, and use a level to ensure level placement. Screw your frame to the wall using 2$\frac{1}{2}$-inch screws.

10. Place wood glue in the screw holes on the box, and slide a dowel rod into the holes. Use a multi-tool to cut off the dowel rod even with the box.

11. Use an orbital sander across all sides of the boards to make sure they're smooth.

12. For a seamless look, apply wood putty in the seams, then let dry before painting.

13. While the wood putty is drying, paint or stain the box and allow it to completely dry, then slide it into place over the frame. Screw the box into the frame using a 2$\frac{1}{2}$-inch wood screw to secure it.

ELEVEN

KITCHEN

When designing your kitchen, remember that this is the heart of your home. If your family is like ours, you will spend a lot of time here. A lot of your budget and time will go toward designing this room, so you will want to make sure it's equally functional and beautiful. Here are some tips and measurements to help you in your design process.

KITCHEN MEASUREMENTS

You will need a minimum of 36 inches between any cabinetry, island, and wall. This not only makes it compliant with the Americans with Disabilities Act standards but also ensures you'll be able to freely move around your kitchen, even while others are in the room. If you have two cabinets facing each other, you can go wider, more like 42 to 48 inches, but anything over 60 inches will be too big.

Lay out your sink, stove, and fridge in the shape of a triangle with a minimum of 4 feet and a maximum of 9 feet on each leg.

A lot of your budget and time will go toward designing this room, so you will want to make sure it's equally functional and beautiful.

The sum of the sides of the triangle should be between 13 and 26 feet. This ensures you can work efficiently and move between your major workstations.

Make sure there is plenty of space wherever your fridge opens. We've seen kitchen designs where the fridge opened right into the area by the stove, and it caused a major bottleneck.

Allow 21 to 36 inches of countertop on either side of your cooktop, and if you put it in your island like we did, make sure to have at least 24 inches from the back of the cooktop to the edge of the island. This keeps little fingers safely away from the cooktop and allows room for people to gather around to visit while you're cooking.

Plan space to put your seasonings, pans, potholders, and cooking utensils near your stove. Put serving ware closer to the dining area, and put everyday glasses and plates closer to the sink.

Any cabinetry over 7 feet high will require a step stool or ladder to reach. We extended ours all the way to our 10-foot ceiling and use the upper areas to store items we use only occasionally.

If you love natural light in your kitchen, install windows. One of the nonnegotiables on Noell's list was a large window over the sink so she could watch our kids playing as she worked in the kitchen.

If you decide to put windows in your kitchen, start your install at 37 inches so that the bottom of the kitchen window would be installed at 37 inches above the ground, if you want it above your countertop. If you want a standard 4-inch backsplash between the countertop and the window, bump it up to 41 inches. If you want a serving window like ours, install it right at your countertop height, which is 36 inches.

Don't be afraid to try new design ideas. For example, we put the oven in the pantry and created a baking station around it. Some people questioned this decision, but we love that it keeps the main kitchen cooler by containing the heat in the pantry and keeps the oven in easy reach when baking bread, cookies, pies, and so on. If you think of something that might be beneficial, don't be afraid to go for it.

Standard Appliance Measurements

Refrigerator measurements:

Standard: 36 inches wide x 30 inches deep

Counter depth varies but less than 30 inches

Stove measurements:

Standard: 30 inches wide x 25–27 inches deep

Dishwasher measurements:

Standard: 24 inches wide x 24 inches deep x 35 inches tall, to fit under the counter

Cabinetry Measurements

Custom cabinetry can be built in any size, but these standards will get you started.

Lowers

Standard height before countertop: 34 inches

With countertop: 35–36 inches

Depth, front to wall without countertop: 24 inches

With countertop: 25–26 inches

Standard widths: 12, 18, 24, 30, 33, 36, and 48 inches

Height between lowers and uppers: 18 inches

Uppers

Standard heights: 30, 36, and 42 inches

Standard depths: 12, 15, 18, and 24 inches

Standard widths: 9–48 inches, in 3-inch increments

Tall Cabinets

Standard heights: 84, 90, and 96 inches

Standard widths: 18, 24, or up to 36 inches

Standard depths: 12 or 24 inches

CABINETRY

There are so many ways to save money on cabinetry. Begin by scouring resell sites, Habitat for Humanity ReStores, or local salvage stores in your area to find perfectly good cabinetry that can be updated with paint and hardware.

We do a lot of restoration work and have pulled perfectly good cabinets out of high-end homes that we either sold for a great price or gave away to family and friends. Get the word out that you are looking for cabinetry, and you may be surprised what you find. If you can't find cabinetry to reuse, you can still save money by using the following tips to purchase new.

One of the least expensive ways to install new cabinetry is to purchase IKEA boxes and add your own semicustom doors that you can find readily available online. And if you prefer more quality boxes, there are plenty of websites that offer semicustom cabinetry.

Here are some tips to save money:

> **Our favorite kitchen additions for storage and organization:**
> Peg system
> Deep drawers
> KitchenAid mixer cabinet
> Spice rack
> Built-in knife holder
> Multilayer drawers
> Cookie sheet organizers

- Choose simple styles. While flat-front cabinets are the cheapest option, shaker style are just a little more expensive and really dress up your cabinetry. You can save money by skipping decorative legs, fancy corbels, glass panels, and fancy crown molding, which can easily be added as a DIY project.
- Choose partial overlay versus full overlay, or inset cabinet doors and drawers.
- Be willing to assemble your cabinetry yourself.
- Choose an affordable wood species. Ask what the most affordable woods are in your region.
- Opt for open shelving. While this is currently trendy, doing it tastefully can save money and offer a timeless style that will last for years to come. You can always add doors later.
- Choose to forgo soft-close, specialty cabinets, and fancy pullouts. You can add the fancy pullouts after the fact.
- Know that doors are cheaper than drawers.
- Incorporate furniture. Rather than paying for a full wall of built-in cabinets, add a hutch or buffet with open shelving over it, or any other piece of furniture you can think of. Remember, think outside the box and use pieces in unexpected ways.

Cabinetry is one thing we chose to splurge on. This went back to our list of nonnegotiables. For us, beautiful cabinetry was a priority. So, we allocated more of our budget here, choosing to skimp in other areas. We worked with a designer out of Indiana, Hilary Denton of Vintage Forward Designs, and she brought all our dreams to life.

COUNTERTOPS

Depending on where you live, porcelain can be a great choice for countertops. We went with SapienStone and could not be happier with our choice.

If you're looking for something a little less expensive, installing tile, butcher block, or reclaimed wood are great options. An amazing DIY option is concrete. We used this in our eldest daughter's bathroom, and it's an inexpensive, easy project that requires very little hands-on time. The hardest part is building the forms, but the countertops can be made in a variety of colors and textures, plus they are durable and beautiful—a perfect option for a kitchen (see "Project: Concrete Countertops" later in this chapter).

MAJOR APPLIANCES AND ACCESSORIES

We've found some great options for saving money on appliances. One time we saved over $3,000 by driving three hours away and purchasing our oven from a secondhand dealer. It was in perfect condition other than a missing handle, which we simply ordered from the manufacturer.

To achieve a high-end look in our kitchen, we went with panel-front appliances and had panels made that matched our cabinetry. The panels cost only $300—so much cheaper than splurging on high-end appliances.

Here are some helpful tips we've learned along the way:

- Start your search early.
- If you can find a great deal, it's worth storing the appliances until you're ready to build.
- You can also shop outlets, look for floor models, or look for scratch-and-dent types of places.
- Search retailer and manufacturer sites for rebates, special offers, and discounts on overstocked items.
- Remember that the best time of year to purchase an appliance is near a holiday, so be patient and wait for those big discounts, if you can.

- Keep an eye out for any type of specialty discount. Some places like Lowe's offer a 10 percent discount for military, and some places may offer contractor pricing if you are building your own home.
- Don't be afraid to negotiate or ask a store to price match.
- Don't be afraid to check your local warehouse club. We found our washer and dryer at Costco.com for much less than it was being sold elsewhere.

Faucets

Before choosing faucets, really consider your budget. Yes, you may be able to find inexpensive faucets on Amazon.com, but think down the road five years. They're not going to last as well and may end up costing more in damage to your kitchen. (Water damage is incredibly expensive to repair.) So again, as in many other situations, weigh your options and decide if this is something you're willing to splurge on or if this is a temporary fix, one that will look amazing for now but may need to be revisited in the future.

Hardware

While individual pulls may not seem super expensive, if your home is anything like ours, you will need hundreds of them throughout. That adds up quickly. Hardware is a great place to save. You can find countless alternatives out there that resemble high-end pulls, which can end up saving you thousands of dollars.

PANTRY

We ended up including our pantry in our cabinetry, as we had fully intended on building it ourselves. Whether you're building your own home or renovating an existing pantry, it's a manageable project that can save you thousands of dollars if you do it yourself, and it will make a difference in your daily living.

Here are some tips that helped us:

- **Make a list.** Think about what types of items you'll be storing in your pantry. Are you the type of person who just brings groceries home and places them on the shelf, or would you rather place them in pretty containers? Will you be storing bulk items, canned goods, small appliances, chip bags, cereal boxes, platters, extra cookware, pet food, paper goods, cookbooks, or cleaning supplies? Make a list of everything you want to make a place for, then start sketching out a design that could work for you.

- **Design your layout.** Vary the height of your shelves to accommodate different-sized packages. Your lower shelves should be the deepest, gradually getting shallower as you reach the top. For bulkier items, make the shelves 18 to 24 inches tall. Shelves for standard groceries should be approximately 14 to 16 inches tall. Smaller 6-inch shelves would be the perfect place to store canned goods and bulk spices.

- **Customize.** The best part about DIYing this is you can design it to the way you like to grocery shop and the way you store pantry goods. You can include space for baskets, jars, trays, and a lazy Susan—there are so many options to add beauty and organization. We love our appliance garage; it keeps our toaster, blender, food processor, and other small appliances neatly tucked out of sight but able to be easily accessed and used. Be sure to include electrical outlets in your pantry if you plan on keeping—and using—small appliances there.

Project

CONCRETE COUNTERTOPS

As mentioned earlier in this chapter, we made this concrete countertop for our daughter's bathroom and love the way it turned out. It's both beautiful and durable—and perfect for a kitchen.

Materials and tools needed:

tape measure
pencil and paper
melamine
painter's tape
table saw
miter saw
silicone
1¹/2- to 2-inch screws (quantity varies depending on the size of your mold)
fondant roller
razor blade or X-Acto knife
round metal shape like a small coffee can
grinder with metal cutting wheel
two long boards, the length of countertop
number 5 rebar
ready-to-mix concrete
water
concrete mixer
concrete pigment (optional)
gloves
hammer
screed board
orbital sander or concrete vibrator
flat trowel
sealer (quantity will depend on the size of your countertop)

Helpful steps for installing concrete countertops:

1. Begin by measuring out your desired countertop dimensions. Measure side to side for length; measure front to back for width; measure side to faucet and sink to ensure correct drain placement.
2. Decide how thick you want the countertop. Generally, 1–1.5 inches is standard thickness, though 2 inches will create a more defined look.
3. Draw out the template on paper.
4. Place measurements on melamine to create the form. Use tape to mark the edges and carefully draw the drain opening measurements.
5. Using the table saw and miter saw, cut out and assemble the melamine form, attaching the sides (anywhere from 1 to 2 inches deep) to the main piece using 1¹/2- to 2-inch screws.
6. Work quickly to apply silicone to all the joints, rolling it smoothly into place using a fondant roller. Silicone dries *fast*, so apply Windex or water to keep it wet a little longer.
7. Use a razor blade to cut off any excess silicone.
8. To form drain holes, use a circular form large enough for your desired drain size. Make sure it is sturdy enough to hold its weight against concrete. (We used small coffee cans.) Set it in place and apply silicone around the edges to keep it from moving.
9. Once your form is built, use the grinder to cut the rebar to fit inside the form, then set aside. These will be used to stabilize the heavy finished countertop and keep it from breaking. These should be placed every 4–8 inches.

10. Place the form on two long boards, then rest those on either a tabletop or sawhorses.

11. Now it's time to begin mixing the concrete. Using a fast-setting concrete will give the countertop a more textured, coquina finish, whereas traditional concrete will create a smoother finish. Mix the concrete mix with water; each 80-pound bag takes about 3 quarts of water. Add the concrete mix first, then slowly add water, mixing continually until it reaches a uniform, workable consistency. If you want the countertop any color besides gray, now is the time to add concrete pigment. Follow the manufacturer's specifications.

12. Begin filling in your form with the wet concrete, about halfway deep. Be sure to wear gloves to protect your hands. Pound it down into the form using your gloved hands, boards, or hammers to ensure it is as compact and airtight as possible.

13. Once your form is halfway full, set the rebar into place, and push it down into the wet concrete.

14. Continue filling the form with concrete on top of the rebar.

15. Once the form is completely full, use a screed board to make it level, and clean off any excess concrete.

16. Have a person stand on either side of the form and grab the two long boards it's sitting on. Now firmly shake it. Use an orbital sander or concrete vibrator and run it along the bottom and edges to get out all the air bubbles and ensure a smooth countertop.

17. Use a flat trowel to pull excess sludge to the front edge of the countertop. You'll want the front of the countertop to be just a little thicker than the back.

18. Let the concrete cure for twenty-four hours inside the form, then remove the sides of the form and let it dry for another forty-eight hours.

19. Once completely dry, remove the rest of the form, and set the countertop into place. These countertops are very heavy, so make sure to have extra hands to help set it into place.

20. To protect the countertop from staining, seal before use with two to three coats of a quality concrete sealer. A matte sealer will offer a more natural look, and if you prefer a glossy finish, go for a glossy sealer.

Tips: We used four 80-pound bags of concrete mix for our 75×21×2-inch countertop. There's a calculator on quikrete.com that can tell you exactly how much you should need. Also, you can rent a mixer at most home improvement stores, or use a drill with paddle attachment, or a wheelbarrow and shovel.

TWELVE

LAUNDRY AND MUDROOM

To save on space, we decided to combine our laundry and mudroom in the same space. While that's not required, when laying out your floor plan, you at least want them to be near each other and preferably near an entrance to the home. This especially comes in handy when entering the house with wet or dirty clothing, outerwear, or shoes. Being able to remove them and immediately place them in the laundry room to be cleaned or stored in a nearby mudroom without traipsing mud and water through the house will make your life so much easier.

Although function is definitely the most important aspect of designing a laundry and mudroom, adding beauty to the design will make these spaces more enjoyable to spend time in, even if the work you're doing might not be your favorite.

> Adding beauty to the design will make these spaces more enjoyable.

LAUNDRY ROOM PLANNING

In your laundry room design, think through what your laundry process looks like, what else you may want to do in this space, and what you plan to store in this room:

- Do you air-dry a lot of clothes? You might want to include drying racks.
- Are your bedrooms on a different level? A laundry chute may be very handy.
- Do you like to separate your laundry as you load the washer, or would you like to have a different spot to separate the laundry beforehand? You may want to include bins or hampers and design cabinetry to store them.
- Will you want to hand-wash or soak laundry? Bathe your pet? You might want to include a laundry room sink.
- Do you want to fold your laundry in the laundry room? Include some type of countertop or table that will give you space to do so.

Be sure to include plenty of storage. Sit down and write out everything you intend to store in your laundry room. For us, we store laundry supplies, cleaning tools and supplies, beach towels, and bulk items like paper towels and toilet paper.

MUDROOM PLANNING

Mudrooms act as a sort of hub of the home, so think about how you want yours to function. For example:

- Do you want to simply store coats and shoes?
- Do you want a locker for each child to have a place to keep things like backpacks and school stuff?
- Do you want wall space to hang a family calendar?
- Do you need storage for things like seasonal items and sports equipment?

In our mudroom, we installed a locker for each child with concealed storage above them (where Noell stored craft supplies and extra vases) and with four large baskets underneath (one for soccer equipment, one for a pool bag, one for shoes, and one as a catchall).

Our laundry and mudroom was not a large room by any stretch of the imagination, so we installed floor-to-ceiling cabinetry and tile to maximize our storage space and make it appear larger than it actually was.

There are many projects throughout this book that you could incorporate into this space—like floating shelves or wallpaper. Here are a couple of our favorite DIY projects from our laundry and mudroom.

Project:

BRICK FLOOR

For our laundry and mudroom combo, we chose to install brick floors as they are durable, easy to clean, and hide dirt. (Pro tip: We also used these same tools and principles to install the brick wall in our bedroom.)

Materials and tools needed:

thin bricks
spacers
thin-set mortar
trowel
grinder
sanded grout
bucket of water
drill
paddle bit
grout bag
sponges
sealer (optional)
painter's tape (optional)
knee pads (optional)

Tip: Just as spacing affects the look, you can completely change the appearance of the brick floor based on *how* you apply the grout and the color you choose. If you barely fill in the joints, you'll have a nice, neat line between bricks, whereas if you use a heavier hand and wipe it across the face of the bricks, you can give the bricks a more white-washed appearance, if using a lighter-colored grout.

Helpful steps for installing a brick floor:

1. Lay out bricks in your desired pattern: straight, herringbone, or brick joint, to name a few. Try to lay out your pattern so you will have as few cuts as possible. The standard is to use 3/8-inch spacers, and you can greatly change the look by going wider or thinner.

2. After you've determined the layout, mix the thin-set mortar, and begin applying it to the floor using a trowel. Work in smaller sections so the thin-set doesn't dry before you can install the brick.

3. Lay down full pieces first, then make all the cuts using your grinder and install them on the perimeter.

4. Once all the bricks are in place on top of the thin-set mortar and you've allowed it to dry overnight, it's time to grout. Place the grout in a bucket and slowly add water, mixing it with a drill and paddle bit until it resembles a thick milkshake. Pour the grout into a grout bag, folding over the tip and firmly holding it in place as you fill the bag to keep the grout from leaking out. (This is similar to decorating a cake with icing.)

5. Begin filling the joints with grout. If you want a more textured finish, allow the grout to dry for about ten minutes, then wipe with a clean sponge and fresh water. You can play with your technique until you're happy with the result.

6. For optimal results, seal the brick floor with a penetrating sealer once the grout is dry. Be sure to apply painter's tape to baseboards, cabinetry, and doors to protect them from the sealer.

Brick floor

Project

MUDROOM LOCKERS

Mudrooms may seem to be a newer trend, but Noell's great-grandparents had a mudroom right off the back porch of their homestead farmhouse that served as a room to take off muddy work boots, do laundry, and store bulk items. We love that this staple from traditional American farmhouses is again finding a place in modern culture. Building mudroom lockers is a great way to create a functional space for your family at a low price point.

Materials and tools needed:

tape measure
pencil
4-foot level
stud finder
¾-inch cabinet-grade plywood (size and quantity depend on your space)
primed 1×2s (size and quantity depend on your space)
sawhorses
paint
paint sprayer
table saw
miter saw
sandpaper
16-gauge nail gun
speed square
torpedo level
18-gauge nail gun
molding (base, shoe, and crown)
caulk
masking tape and paper

Helpful steps for building mudroom lockers:

1. Begin by sketching out a plan to offer an idea of the overall layout. Carefully consider the size of the items that you would like to organize and plug those numbers into your sketch. This will assist you in designing a system that will be most functional for your family and lifestyle.

2. Determine how many cubbies you would like. Measure the width of your space and divide the width by the number of cubbies desired. For example, if you have a 60-inch space and you want four cubbies, divide 60 inches by four; this means each cubby will have a 15-inch width. Based on your equally divided number, place a mark on the wall to signify where the main dividers will land. Using a level and a pencil, make a vertical plumb line on these marks.

3. Determine the height of your base. If your intention is to be able to sit down to take off your shoes, for instance, that height should be somewhere between 16 and 20 inches. Using a level and pencil, mark a level line on the back wall at the desired base height.

4. Determine the overall height that you want the system to be. Mark a level line at that height.

5. Use a stud finder, and mark these with an *X* along the level lines for both the height of the base and the overall height of the system.

6. Determine how deep your system will be for the seating and locker

Other tools as needed:

air compressor
air hose
finish nailer
hammer
nail punch
wood glue
clamps
1¼-inch finish nails
sponge
bucket of water

space. (We chose 18 inches for ours to allow for a deeper area for seating at the base of our built-in, and our lockers above are 12 inches deep.)

7. Once you have a general idea of where everything will go and how large your system is, put a materials and quantity list together and then head to your local home improvement store. Depending on your preference, you may want to have one piece of plywood cut into those 18-inch-deep sections for the sides and shelving.

8. It's easiest to paint a primer coat on the plywood and trim prior to installation. When you get home, set up a paint-spraying station using sawhorses. Lay out all your wood and with the use of your battery-powered sprayer, paint two coats on both sides of the boards. Allow adequate dry time, and sand between each coat. This step will save you hours of hand painting at awkward angles or in hard-to-reach spaces.

9. While the exterior pieces are drying, install the supports. Begin by using a table saw to cut a 1×2 to fit the length of the system's base, and attach it along the level line with a 16-gauge nail gun, making sure to hit each stud that should've been marked earlier. Then do the same for the very top. The 1×2s will act as the wall support for the back of the top shelf.

10. Next, cut a 1×2 piece for the left- and right-hand sides of the adjoining walls. For the base, cut these roughly 17 inches long (just a bit shorter than the depth of the bench); for the sides of the upper shelves, cut them roughly 11 inches long (for the depth of the lockers).

11. Now, cut one of the 18-inch-wide plywood pieces to fit the space allowed for the top of the base, and set it in place.

12. Measure from the floor up to the bottom of your base. Cut two to three 18-inch dividers (depending on how many cubbies you'd like). This creates tidy storage for shoes or baskets and adds necessary support. Slide in each piece where you made the vertical marks. Square up the wood using a speed square, then nail

from the top. Plumb the newly placed plywood pieces with your torpedo level, and tack a nail at the bottom of each piece.

13. Now cut one of the 12-inch plywood pieces to fit the space allowed for the top shelf, and set it in place.

14. Measure from the bottom of your top shelf to the top of your base. Take that measurement and cut two to three pieces (depending on the number of cubbies) of the 12-inch-wide plywood material to fit the space.

15. Slide in each piece for the locker sides and dividers where you previously made the vertical marks. Square up the wood using a speed square, then nail from the top. Plumb the newly placed plywood pieces with your 4-foot level and tack a nail at the bottom of each piece.

16. Now that the main portion of your system is done, it's time to install the trim. Start with the base molding. Use an 18-gauge nail gun for this part. Cut each piece to fit in between the dividers. Repeat the same process with the shoe molding.

17. Next, install the 1×2 trim pieces along the edges of all the plywood to secure the system.

18. Then, cut and fit the decorative crown molding piece into place and nail.

19. Now it's time to caulk and paint the system. (After building several of these, we learned that it's easier to use a battery-operated sprayer to do the final topcoat of paint, rather than paint it by hand. Yes, there is more prep work to do to eliminate overspray, but it will still be a big time-saver in the end. So, mask off the floor, walls, and doors and get to spraying.)

THIRTEEN

BEDROOMS

———

When designing your bedrooms, you are creating safe havens of rest and relaxation, dreamy retreats that allow your family to rejuvenate, renew, and restore in a peaceful environment that has been carefully curated to match their individual styles. A bedroom should be free of clutter, offer plenty of organization, and provide a calm atmosphere for reading, resting, and relationships.

For each room, you'll want to draw from the other chapters in this book to determine the style, wall treatments, and lighting fixtures, and consider not only how you plan to use these rooms, but also how you want to *feel* in these rooms. Whether serene, cozy, romantic, or inspired, you can create your desired outcome with just a bit of envisioning and planning.

In this chapter, we've kept the main concepts fairly simple and have included several DIY projects that you can try for yourself or that might inspire you to create your own innovative and creative solutions.

> Whether serene, cozy, romantic, or inspired, you can create your desired outcome with just a bit of envisioning and planning.

PRIMARY BEDROOM

Tip: To achieve the look of our brick statement wall, use the same materials and instructions for the "Brick Floor" project in chapter 12, "Laundry and Mudroom."

When designing our main bedroom during our build from the ground up, we wanted a space that felt cozy and comfortable, evoking a spirit that was warm and inviting versus having a big room with lots of wasted space and that might also feel overwhelming. We have been in many main bedrooms that were big—just for the sake of being big—and the resulting space did not feel inviting.

We measured out the furniture we planned to put in the room, added space to comfortably move around, and created a perfectly cozy room. We incorporated a brick accent wall for texture, painted the remaining walls in a soothing gray, and chose an elegant chandelier paired with nightstand lamps for lighting. We opted for an upholstered headboard and then layered our bed with soft textiles. The large apothecary cabinet as our dresser added a warm, rustic touch.

If you're renovating an existing space on a limited budget, no problem. You can still achieve your desired effect by sticking to some design basics, perhaps by simply changing wall coverings and lighting.

Tip: For a super-easy DIY, we made our daughter Aisley's bed by placing a piece of plywood cut to fit on top of three Ikea Kallax bookcases, arranged in a *U* shape. With its built-in storage, this bed is perfect for any small space, and it's great for adding instant interest. Especially with the floor-level storage, little ones can easily access books and toys. String fairy lights using pushpins or thumbtacks, and place cozy pillows under the bed for an extra-special touch.

ADDITIONAL BEDROOMS

For you, an additional bedroom might be designed for the occasional random guest, or for a specific guest who regularly visits, or maybe for a family member who has come to live with you full time. Or possibly

you rent out an extra bedroom—either long or short term—and want to help create special experiences for people by adding inspired special touches.

For us, our additional bedrooms are designed with our children in mind. If you're like us and want to create spaces kids would love, we've included some of the things we did for our children's rooms to add extra-special touches that you can add to any additional bedroom.

CLOSET SYSTEMS

Closet systems all too often seem to get overlooked. They typically don't provide the glitz and glamour of a bathroom or a kitchen, but when it comes to keeping your family organized and functional, they are important and affect day-to-day living. If you've ever priced out a custom closet system, you

know how expensive they are, even the ones made from particle board. For a comparable, if not lower, price, you can build a system that perfectly meets your family's needs from products that will last.

The great thing about designing and building your own closet system is you can design it to exactly fit the needs of the person who will be using it. For example, a toddler will not need a lot of long hanging space but rather small cubbies where their little clothes can be perfectly folded and organized. A teen girl might not wear a lot of long dresses, but she may have a massive shoe collection she needs to organize. Another child may wear a lot of athletic clothes and would prefer baskets over additional hanging space, so you might want to include more cubbies for baskets than hanging rods. And for a guest room, a simple shelf or two and a standard wooden rod might suffice for hanging clothes.

Note: The bases of our closets are made from 3/4-inch cabinet-grade plywood. Most bedroom closets will not require more than two to three sheets. If you're shopping at Home Depot or Lowe's, they have a large industrial saw on site and will cut the plywood to size for you. Have them cut four equal pieces of each 4×8 sheet longways; the measurement will be just shy of 12 inches, taking into account the size of the blade. This is a big time-saver and will ensure that you get smooth, even cuts throughout.

Project:

SIMPLE CANOPY

Canopies make any room extra dreamy, so we couldn't resist adding one to our daughter's room. They aren't exclusive to bedrooms, though. Place a canopy over a couch or reading chair to create an extra-cozy space, or install one over a small bistro table to add a touch of romance and create magical dining experiences.

Materials and tools needed:

greenery garland
a round metal hoop in your
    desired diameter (you can
    find these at home decor
    supply stores)
twine or jute
lace curtains
fishing wire or invisible hang-
    ing wire
screw or hook

Helpful steps for installing a canopy:

1. Secure garland around the hoop using twine or jute to attach.
2. Attach curtains to the hoop using fishing wire, tying in four different spots, allowing the hoop to perfectly balance.
3. Gather the fishing wire lines together and wrap them around a screw or hook that is driven into the ceiling, preferably into a joist.

Project:

WOODEN SWING

Want to see someone instantly smile when they walk into a room? Add a swing, preferably a wooden one. Whether for a child's bedroom, an adult's bedroom, a guest room, or maybe even a living area, add a touch of whimsy and bring an element of joy to any room by installing a wooden swing. Just be sure to allow room for swinging and use sturdy materials.

Materials and tools needed:

palm sander
wood plank (cut to your
   desired size)
drill with circular bit
sandpaper
paint or stain, if desired
eye screws
stud finder
cotton rope
level

Helpful steps for installing a swing:

1. Sand the board until completely smooth.
2. Cut a 1-inch hole in the center of each side using a circular bit. Smooth out these cuts with sandpaper.
3. Paint or stain if desired and let dry completely. Install eye screws into the ceiling, making sure to get them into the joists for stability. Find these by using a stud finder.
4. Thread cotton rope through the 1-inch holes, tying a tight knot underneath.
5. Attach rope to the eye screws, using a level on the swing to ensure it is straight.

Project

PLATFORM BED

The sky is the limit with this project. If you can dream it, you can build it. Pictures will help your project take shape, but be careful not to bite off more than you can chew. If you have any parts that will be painted, it's best to prime and even apply topcoats prior to install. This way your finished painting will be minimized. The main section consists of a plywood platform, and depending on the size of your space, you may need to add supports underneath. Ours happened to fit snugly within three walls. Also, depending on the height of the platform, take into consideration the potential need for safety railing.

Materials and tools needed:

pencil
level
stud finder
tape measure
support beam (necessary if
    using only two walls)
2×4s
sliding compound miter saw
impact drill
3-inch screws
circular saw
plywood

Other tools as needed:

air compressor
16-gauge nail gun
1×2s

Helpful steps for installing a platform bed:

1. Start with marking a level line across your back wall at the desired height of your platform.

2. Use a stud finder to find and mark the studs on all three walls. (If your space is shaped such that you're using two walls, you'll need to create additional support for the open third side.)

3. Cut 2×4s to fit the space, and then attach them at the stud points using an impact driver and 3-inch screws.

4. Using the circular saw, cut the 3/4-inch plywood base to fit and set on top of the 2×4 support frame. Place mattress and bedding on top.

5. With the use of wood, galvanized piping, or metal, install safety railing.

6. Optional: Build and attach a ladder or add some flair by building a rock wall. (This is easier than it looks. We created a secured ramp made of 3/4-inch plywood and attached a set of various-shaped rock-climbing holds per the manufacturer's recommendations.)

CHALKBOARD DOORS

Ideally, you'll want to use a one- or two-panel door for this project. If you already have a door with more panels, you can simply use plywood cut slightly smaller than your door and adhere with liquid nails. Add chair railing to frame it. Or you can also simply paint the inside or outside of your child's closet door to give them a fun space to be creative. Have fun writing inspiring quotes on it, write their daily or weekly schedule, or use it as a teaching tool by allowing them to practice math or writing skills on it.

Materials and tools needed:

one- or two-panel door
painter's tape
plywood (optional, see head-
   note description above)
paintbrush or roller
magnetic primer
chalkboard paint
chalk
eraser or soft cloth
finish nailer (optional)
chair railing, cut to size of
   chalkboard frame (optional)

Helpful steps for creating chalkboard doors:

1. Tape off any parts of the door you don't want to paint.

2. Prime the door (or plywood) with magnetic paint.

3. Allow the primer time to dry, then paint with chalkboard paint.

4. Prime the chalkboard area by rubbing chalk all over it and then wiping away with an eraser or soft cloth.

5. Option: For a special touch, use a finish nailer to attach a chair railing to the frame.

Chalkboard doors

you
can ♥

CLOSET SYSTEM

Carefully consider the wardrobe of the person who will be using each closet and design a system that will be most functional for them, sketching it out first to offer an idea of the overall layout. You might want to collect some measurements of items such as dress lengths or shoe and boot heights and plug the numbers into your sketch. If you're creating this for children, don't forget to take into consideration how quickly they can grow, so allow room for their bigger shoes and longer pants in years to come. If you really want to include some of the fancier inserts from IKEA, build your cubes to their standard sizes so you can incorporate their drawers, jewelry organizers, or pant hangers.

Materials and tools needed:

tape measure
4-foot level
pencil
stud finder
3/4-inch cabinet-grade
    plywood
primed 1×2s
primed 1×6s
paint sprayer (battery powered
    is preferred)
sawhorses
paint
16-gauge nail gun
miter saw
speed square
molding (base, shoe, and
    crown)
18-gauge nail gun
hanging rods and brackets
caulk
various-sized nails
masking tape and paper

Helpful steps for building a closet system:

1. Take measurements and sketch a general plan on paper.

2. Determine the overall height that you want the closet system to be. Using a level and pencil, mark a level line at that height. Continue to measure and mark level lines where any additional shelves and dividers will go, based on your drawings and measurements.

3. While you're there, use a stud finder to mark an *X* on each stud along your horizontal lines.

4. Put a materials quantity list together and head to your local home improvement store.

5. It's easiest to paint a primer coat on the plywood and trim prior to installation. When you get home, set up a paint-spraying station using sawhorses. Lay out all the wood and with the use of a battery-powered sprayer, paint two coats on both sides of your boards. Make sure to allow adequate dry time between each coat. This step will save you hours of painstaking, awkward angle painting.

6. Where you marked a level line at the top of your system, install the first 1×2 in place using a 16-gauge nail gun, and nail into studs as often as possible. This will act as the wall support for the back of

the top shelf. Also attach a 1×6 piece on the left- and right-hand sides of the adjoining walls, roughly 11 inches in length.

7. Now cut one of your plywood pieces to fit the space allowed (96 inches for ours) for the top shelf and set in place.

8. Next, measure from the bottom of your top shelf to the floor. Take that measurement (72–84 inches for ours) and cut two pieces of the 12-inch-wide plywood material to fit the space.

9. Measure the center point of the top shelf, and then measure to the right 12 inches and to the left 12 inches, giving a total of a 24-inch-wide center shelf.

10. Slide in each piece where you made the 12-inch marks and square it up using a speed square, then nail from the top. Using your level, plumb the newly placed plywood pieces and tack a nail at the bottom of each piece. Now that the main pieces are installed, you can start installing the center parts to the shelving system.

11. Cut five pieces of plywood at 24 inches in length.

12. Install the shelving from the bottom up at 12-inch increments. You can customize this height to fit your design.

13. On the left side of the space, mark a level line at 36 inches in height. Install another 1×2 for support of your shelf on that line.

14. Also add another horizontal 12-inch support on both the wall and the vertical plywood to the right.

15. Measure, cut, and install your plywood for your secondary shoe rack (36 inches).

16. Now the base of your system is done, and it's time to install the trim. Start with the base molding and shoe molding. You can use your 18-gauge nail gun for this part. Cut each piece to fit all the way around the closet including the center shelving piece by mitering the edges. Repeat the same process with your shoe molding.

17. Next, install the 1×2 trim pieces on the edges of all the plywood.

18. Now, cut and fit the decorative crown molding piece into place and nail.

19. Install hanging rods with their respective mounting brackets.

20. Now it's time to caulk and paint the system. After building several of these, we learned that it's easier to use our battery-operated sprayer to apply the final topcoat of paint, rather than paint it by hand. Yes, there is more prep work to do to eliminate overspray, but it will still be a big time-saver in the end. So, mask off the floor, walls, and the doors and get to spraying.

FOURTEEN

BATHROOMS

When designing our main bathroom, we wanted to create a spa-like feel—a space we could relax in and rejuvenate after a long day. While we see many people eliminating bathtubs, we wanted ours to be front and center. We both enjoy soaking in the tub, and our kids think taking a bath is the answer to all the world's problems.

> You do not have to have a massive bathroom full of grandeur to make a statement.

Feeling sick? Momma will pour you a detox bath.

Feeling upset? Momma will pour you a calming bath.

Having problems falling asleep? Momma will pour you a relaxing bath.

So, a nice big soaking tub was a priority for our family. Whether you want to create an oasis, or you just want a functional yet beautiful bathroom, here are some things to think about incorporating.

CREATING A FOCAL POINT

A focal point . . . for the bathroom? Yes.

Every house has a bathroom. What makes yours special? What can be done to make yours unique?

This can be achieved by introducing a focal point, a piece that creates a "wow" factor. It could be in the form of an accent wall, a chandelier, mosaics, a unique vanity, or maybe even the view. It needs to be bold and immediately capture the attention of anyone who views the space.

Though our bathroom is a modest size, by adding slabs of porcelain to the back wall, making our shower a focal point, and centering the soaking tub outside of it with a dynamic glass chandelier hanging above, we made it appear much larger and more grand. You do not have to have a massive bathroom full of grandeur to make a statement. When done properly, even the most humble of bathrooms can feel magnificent.

STATEMENT SHOWER AND TUB

To design a shower that makes a statement, make it as large as you feel comfortable making it. Tile is beautiful, but using frameless glass will make your shower feel larger. If possible, eliminate the shower curb for a cleaner, more modern look that is safer as well.

Though we could not eliminate our shower curbs, we hid them behind the knee wall so it looked curbless from the front. Make sure to include niches—we like to place them out of sight to give the shower a cleaner appearance—and also include a bench to give you a place to sit and enjoy your new, beautiful shower.

If you would like a tub in your design, consider making it part of the focal point. There are so many gorgeous tubs available, and they can be additionally dressed up with faucets. We used a Signature Hardware kitchen faucet set on our primary bathtub because we wanted a wall-mounted faucet with a spray handle, and this one fit what we were envisioning more than any of the other bathtub faucets we were finding. Not a single person ever realized it was a kitchen faucet. So, as we have said many other times, don't be afraid to think outside of the box to bring your dreams to reality.

FOCAL POINTS

If you're remodeling an already-existing bathroom, here are some simple ideas for adding a focal point.

- **Let your tile do the talking.** Choose a simple tile for the majority of the bathroom, then choose a tile with either a unique design, a bold color, or a texture to draw the eye. This can be done in a

ARE MY SUNSHINE
ONLY SUNSHINE
U MAKE ME HAPPY
EN SKIES ARE GREY
U'LL NEVER KNOW DEAR
W MUCH I LOVE YOU
EASE DON'T TAKE
L SUNSHINE AWAY

shower, or you can tile a feature wall. We love adding tile to the wall behind the vanity. You can also incorporate a mosaic tile or tile motif into your design to add a pop of color and drama.

- **Dress your walls.** Add wallpaper or use a bold paint color.
- **Add flair.** Find a unique antique piece that can be used as your vanity, choose fixtures that are interesting, or add a lighting fixture with flair. Choose a countertop that adds an interesting vibe to your space; it can be made of concrete, butcher block, or a slab of wood, perhaps—anything that will draw your eye to it and elevate your space. Just remember that you will use your countertops daily (most likely) and may have different items such as lotions, beauty products, or toothpaste come in contact with them, so make sure to choose a durable surface.

STORAGE

Because our main bathroom is a little on the smaller side, our storage options were limited. We knew that utilizing vertical space is the best way to maximize storage, so we built a leaning tower over our toilet that allowed us to set three baskets on it—the perfect place to store toilet paper, towels, and decorative items like bath salts and candles. You could also install floating shelves, hang baskets or crates from the wall or towel bars, add shelving to any open space, or add any vertical storage piece you can find. Remember: baskets, bins, and hooks are your best friends.

HALF BATHS

A powder room, also commonly called a *half bath*, is the perfect place to have some fun. Because a half bath is generally a smaller space, it is the perfect place to experiment with a bold paint color, a vibrant wallpaper, unique vanities, and seasonal décor. We chose to paint ours Tricorn Black from Sherwin-Williams, which really allows the gold lighting, faucet, and accents to pop. If you end up not liking it or want to change it up, it's a small enough space that it will not feel overwhelming to update it.

LIGHTING

If you are designing a new home, incorporating natural lighting in some way to every space, including bathrooms, will make it so much easier to design beautiful spaces. If you have privacy concerns, place smaller windows up high, and if you're limited on wall space, don't be afraid to place a window in your actual shower. It is truly amazing how much beauty a little natural light can bring to a simple shower.

> Use your lighting as a statement piece to elevate your design.

If you have a bathroom that has no natural lighting, it's important to consider what that bathroom will be used for. If you'll be applying makeup and getting ready, design a lighting plan that will be flattering and not create harsh shadows in the mirror. A great solution to this is to install an LED mirror that has even lighting from all sides. If you are working on a powder room or other bathroom that's not used for getting ready, you can use your lighting as a statement piece to elevate your design.

Following are some important things to remember regarding bathroom lighting:

- Like pretty much every other space, you need to have layers of lighting.
- Ambient lighting will be chandeliers, pendants, recessed and flush mounts, task lighting for your makeup application or grooming, and accent lighting to highlight your decor or architectural features.
- Some bathroom lighting can serve as more than one layer; for example, sconces beside your mirror highlight your decor and also serve as task lighting.
- Bathrooms are a great place to put your lights on dimmer switches so you can easily control the ambience of the room.
- Make sure the recessed lighting in your shower is moisture rated if it will only be exposed to humidity or damp rated if it will actually come in contact with water.

For lighting on either side of your mirror, which is the best lighting to reduce shadows, hang your fixtures 36 to 40 inches apart and approximately 60 to 66 inches from the floor. If you have a wider mirror, placing your lighting above the mirror is the next best place. If you really want to eliminate harsh shadows, choose a light that is at least 24 inches wide and covered with an opaque cover. Ideally, it should be approximately 78 inches above the floor.

Though personal taste is more important than any hard-and-fast rules, here are some general sizing guidelines:

- The width of a single light fixture above the mirror should equal about a third of the mirror width. For a bar light, calculate 75 percent of your mirror width and choose a light that is that approximate length.
- For a small bathroom, look for sconces that are around 12 inches.
- For a medium bathroom, look for sconces that are around 18 inches.
- For a large bathroom, choose anything over 19 inches.

Note: While a stunning chandelier over a bathtub creates quite the dramatic look, there are some things to consider. The National Electrical Code requires a minimum of 8 feet between the lowest point of the chandelier and the highest point of the bathtub sides. However, your local building codes may be stricter or could completely ban this altogether. Make sure to do some investigation or speak with a licensed electrician before you get your heart completely set on this look.

MAXIMIZING SPACE

When it comes to a bathroom remodel, we find that the biggest thing people are looking for is more space—whether that space is headroom in the shower, storage for their belongings, or just room to move around without stepping on each other while getting ready. How do you make a bathroom feel bigger if you can't change the footprint?

Here are some of the things we've done for clients over the years that you might want to consider for your own bathroom remodel:

- Remove drop ceilings to make showers taller.
- Turn tub surrounds into walk-in showers by removing the bathtub.
- Remove old large, built-in tubs that take up the entire corner and replace them with free-standing soaking tubs.

- Pull out large, awkward vanities and replace them with ones that are better designed to provide more storage while also taking up less space.
- Replace swinging doors with barn doors to create more wall space to use for vertical storage.
- Cut out drywall in between studs and add built-in shelving.
- Add large niches or shelving to your shower for product storage.
- In general, be creative with your design to really maximize your space.

While moving your plumbing does add to the cost and time you will spend on a bathroom remodel, sometimes it is necessary to completely move the shower to a different wall or frame in a new door to make the best use of the space.

When we remodeled our neighbors' bathroom, we removed the existing shower surround, framed in the entryway, and turned what had been the entryway into a walk-in shower. We reframed the doorway on what had been a wall of the shower, moved the vanity to the opposite wall, and flipped the toilet. It was so much more work than if we had just replaced old material in its existing place, but the final product was a much better layout and felt like a much larger, more functional space for their four kids.

Project:

FLOATING WOOD PLANK VANITY

This is the perfect opportunity to find and use reclaimed wood or unique wooden slabs that don't seem to fit in other rooms. Floating wood plank vanities are especially great for smaller spaces like a half bath.

Materials and tools needed:

wooden slab of your choice
Bora-Care
paintbrush
stain
sandpaper
polyurethane
drill
#5 rebar
epoxy
rubber mallet
level
circular drill bit

Helpful steps for installing a floating wood plank vanity:

1. Find a local sawmill and choose a wooden slab that fits the dimensions and look you want. We chose a pecky cypress slab, approximately 18 inches by 14 inches in size, but any wood variety and size will work.

2. Spray the slab with Bora-Care according to the manufacturer's directions to prevent any bug infestations.

3. Next, apply stain with a paintbrush, letting it completely dry and lightly sanding between coats.

4. Before installing, use a paintbrush to coat the slab with polyurethane to protect against water damage.

5. Drill holes into the wall and the back of the vanity top large enough to fit the rebar.

6. Fill holes with epoxy and then push the rebar down into the holes on the vanity top, ensuring you have enough rebar sticking out to properly anchor into the wall. (We used 3-inch rebar.)

7. Push the rebar into the wall, using a rubber mallet to ensure a tight fit.

8. Place a level on the slab to make sure it is level, making adjustments as necessary.

9. Let cure as directed. Use a 3-inch circular drill bit to cut a hole in the center for your drain.

FIFTEEN

HOME OFFICE

Whether building new construction or renovating a home, analyzing your family's needs to see what type of office spaces you'll need in your home is the first step in creating the perfect environment for a quiet, peaceful space that will allow uninterrupted work. Over the past years, this has become even more important as more and more adults are working from home and more families are homeschooling.

You don't always have to have an entire room set aside as an office; sometimes it can be a corner of a room, a part of a closet, or even outside the main house—in the garage or a detached shed.

A home office is a great place to make bold design choices, showcase interests and personalities, and pull in statement pieces.

Because we homeschool, we need a space specifically for doing schoolwork and storing our homeschool materials. Rather than taking up an entire room, we partitioned off part of our room over the garage to make an 8-foot-by-16-foot room, then enclosed one end of it for a materials closet.

A home office is a great place to make bold design choices, showcase interests and personalities, and pull in statement pieces. For ours, we chose a deep, masculine vibe, painting our walls dark navy with Sherwin-Williams Naval, then adding picture frame molding and painted trim for added dimension.

Other options to design an amazing home office on a budget include building or sourcing your desk and adding an inexpensive modern wood accent wall or DIY built-in bookcases.

DESK OPTIONS

Rather than splurging on an expensive desk, think of ways you could use something unexpected.

What makes an office an office? Mainly . . . a desk.

Rather than splurging on an expensive desk, think of ways you could use something unexpected. We used an old dining room table Noell had picked up from an estate sale. Place a piece of glass over the top to make it an even surface for writing. You can easily search online for countless ideas for hacking IKEA furniture, utilizing hairpin legs, creating a wall-mounted desk, or placing a beautiful plank of wood over a filing cabinet or sawhorses to make a desk that will work perfectly in your space for a great price.

Tip: You can use the same principles from both our mudroom lockers (see chapter 12) and our closet systems (see chapter 13) to make custom built-in bookshelves for your office—or for anywhere else in your home.

STUDY NOOK

For our daughter's study nook, we modified a small space—specifically, the inside of her closet—and went with a soft pink and fresh whites to really bring light into an otherwise darker area that had no natural lighting. It's a simple project—one that can be as easy as placing a piece of plywood across two filing cabinets, if space allows. We opted for a slightly different option, and this was the result.

Materials and tools needed:

tape measure
pencil
level
primed plywood (sized to fit
    space of desktop and any
    shelving)
table saw
sliding compound miter saw
1×2 primed trim
16-gauge nail gun
18-gauge nail gun
crown molding (optional)
piano hinge
pegboard
caulk
paint
paintbrush or paint sprayer

Other tools as needed:

speed square
torpedo level
2- and 4-foot levels

Helpful steps for creating a study nook:

1. For the shelving above the desk, measure the space in which you want to add storage. Determine how many shelves you wish to include based on the storage and organization necessary. With a tape measure, pencil, and level, mark out the spacing of the plywood shelf bases.

2. Cut the primed plywood to size with a table saw and sliding compound miter saw. We chose to make the shelves relatively shallow (8 inches deep) for ease of accessibility.

3. Use a 1×2 primed trim for bracing the plywood on the left and right sides of your space. Cut to size, and install with the 16-gauge nail gun.

4. Place the precut plywood pieces on top of the 1×2 bracing and fasten from the top with the 16-gauge nail gun.

5. Cut and install 1×2 primed trim with an 18-gauge nail gun on the face of the plywood as well as the sides to give the shelves a built-in look. (You can also add crown molding at the top if you wish.)

6. For the desk, measure the space and mark out the height at which the bottom of the desk will be. The typical desk height is 28–30 inches. However, we chose to build ours lower to accommodate our daughter's size.

7. Measure and cut the primed plywood to size for the desk base (24 inches deep in our case).

8. Measure and cut the primed 1×2 wood trim to be used as bracing with a sliding compound miter saw. Install this bracing on all three sides of the space where it connects to the wall.

9. Place the primed plywood on top of the 1×2 bracing, and attach from the top using the 16-inch nail gun.

10. Measure and cut the plywood for the sides and back of your desktop with a table saw and sliding compound miter saw. (We chose a draft table–style top, so it was necessary to cut the sides on an angle and the back piece straight.)

11. Install the side pieces on top of the plywood, and attach to the wall using a 16-gauge nail gun. Install the back piece after the sides are in place.

12. Measure and cut the plywood for the face of your desktop to the desired height (3–4 inches).

13. Install this piece by fastening it into the plywood base and sides from the front with an 18-gauge nail gun.

14. On the rear of the desk, measure and cut a piece of plywood that runs the width of your space and is roughly 4 inches deep. Install this piece from the top down with a 16-gauge nail gun.

15. Measure and cut the plywood for the top of your desk. This piece will be the only functional/movable piece of the desk; therefore, it will need to be cut a minimum of a quarter-inch shy of the overall width of the space. This way it doesn't hit the wall when opened. Once cut to fit, install one side of the piano hinge to the back edge of the plywood. Fasten this piece by attaching the other side of the piano hinge to the previous 4-inch-deep plywood piece installed.

16. For the pegboard portion, measure the distance between the top of the desk and the bottom of the shelving. Then cut two pieces of 1×2 trim with a miter saw and install one on each side of the back wall vertically with a 16-gauge nail gun.

17. Cut the pegboard with a table saw to fit the space, and install it using an 18-gauge nail gun.

18. Caulk and paint. Do _not_ caulk the edges of the functional piece of the desktop. It will be inoperable if caulked.

SIXTEEN

DOORS AND WINDOWS

T he front door welcomes people into your home, so it's a perfect place to add some beauty along with hints of your own style and personality. Keeping the front door beautifully decorated with seasonal wreaths and welcome mats is a simple way to refresh your home's look.

Windows are more than just glass to allow natural light to shine through. There's as much window variety as there are architectural styles.

In choosing our window design, we wanted to match the simplicity of the farmhouse style, staying true to styles that would have

> The architectural style of your home can dictate the style of window you choose, but feel free to go with whatever style you love.

been installed in the old farmhouses across the heartland of America. The architectural style of your home can dictate the style of window you choose, but feel free to go with whatever style you love. Personally, we like the cleaner look of fewer windowpanes as it allows for a clearer view of the great outdoors.

But first, let's talk about the foundation of creating a beautiful door for that wreath to hang on and that welcome mat to be placed beneath.

DESIGN

Painting your door is a great way to freshen your frontage.

If you're building from scratch, don't forget to use all the shopping and sourcing techniques we mentioned earlier in the book. But if you're renovating or looking for a little face-lift, painting your door is a great way to freshen your frontage.

When building from the ground up, door and window selections will be incredibly important for your overall aesthetic. These utilitarian items are anything but, and they have as many unique and distinct design elements as there are different architectural designs.

If you'd like to stay true to an architectural style, do your research to make sure the windows you like will fit or complement your overall aesthetic.

Project:

DOOR INSTALLATION

While many renovations will not require door installations, if you are building new construction or doing a major remodel, you may find yourself needing to install additional doors or change out existing ones. It can be very time-consuming to ensure your doors are perfectly installed, but taking the time to do it right will ensure minimal frustrations in the future with sagging doors or doors that stick or squeak.

Materials and tools needed:

door (sized to fit your entry or
    frame)
tape measure
reciprocating saw
15- or 16-gauge nail gun
15- to 16-gauge 2-inch finish nails
level
shims, wood or composite
caulk
3- to 4-inch construction screws
window tape
spray-foam insulation

Other tools as needed:

hammer
seam tape
impact driver

Note: For both interior and exterior doors, frame up the rough opening. This should be at least 2 inches larger on all sides. Use a reciprocating saw to make the opening larger if needed. Check for plumbness of both your wall and door jambs, and then ensure the floor is level.

Helpful steps for installing an interior prehung door:

1. Typically, a split-faced, prehung interior hollow-core door is lightweight enough to use a nail gun only. However, it's perfectly fine to use screws as fasteners. For anything heavier, we recommend predrilling holes and using screws.

2. Check rough openings. They should be 2 inches larger than the prehung door jamb. Ideally, you want at least a 1-inch clearance on both sides to ensure you can properly plumb the door. It's okay if your clearance is slightly smaller, but if you have little to no clearance, you may need to trim with a reciprocating saw or, worst-case scenario, reframe the opening.

3. Make sure the swing of the door is facing the correct direction per your plans.

4. As you put the door into place, make sure the outside of your jamb is flush with the drywall on both sides.

5. Using a nail gun, tack the door into place with one nail, starting on the hinge side.

6. Use a level to ensure plumbness and add shims as needed.

7. As you add fasteners or shims, make sure your jamb remains plumb by constantly checking it with your level. Open the door to make sure the reveal between your jamb and the door is equal all the way around. If not, adjust accordingly with shims.

8. While the door is still open, make sure it does not swing farther open or close by itself. If it does, you may need to check the plumbness of your door again. A properly installed door should not swing by itself. Also, make sure the door opens and closes freely.

9. Finish adding fasteners in the casing, starting at the hinges.

Helpful steps for installing an exterior door:

1. If your house has a wood subfloor, you may need to research your local building codes for exterior door applications. Most municipalities will simply require 6-inch window tape applied directly to the door opening floor and wrapped up the studs 8 inches. However, some may require a metal pan. Either way, or if your house is built on a concrete slab, simply apply a heavy bead of caulk (at least a half-tube, if not a full tube) to the bottom of the door opening.

2. Now repeat the same steps as the interior door requires. The exterior doors do not give the flexibility for fastener types. Code will likely require screws only.

3. Once your door is installed, open and close it to check functionality.

4. Now flash your door correctly to keep water out. Install 4-inch window tape on both sides of the doorjamb, overlapping the jamb 1/4 inch.

5. Next, install your window tape on the top of the door, overlapping existing tape by at least 1/2 inch.

6. If this is new construction, insulating around the door will be done with the rest of the house. For a remodel, you need to insulate between the jamb and your rough framing. We recommend using a can of spray-foam insulation.

Project:

WINDOW INSTALLATION

We were quoted over $3,000 for our window installations—this is for installation alone, not including the windows—and they projected it would take them less than a day. We were able to complete this project in less than two days, and it would have been even faster if we hadn't had to use the man lift for our higher windows. In the end, we were able to save the $3,000 and put it toward something else.

Materials and tools needed:

tape measure
window
reciprocating saw
house wrap
caulk gun and caulk
2.5- to 3-inch pan head screws
level
shims
electric screwdriver
a man lift or extension ladders, depending on the height of your home
window tape
seam tape

Other tools as needed:

hammer
impact driver

Tip: Before installing your window, make sure to check that your weather-resistant barrier and windowsill flashing are installed correctly, are up to code for your local area, and are not damaged or compromised in any way.

Helpful steps for installing a window:

1. Begin by using a tape measure to measure your opening top to bottom and side to side at at least two different points. Measure your window to make sure space allotted is adequate. If not, use a reciprocating saw to widen the opening.

2. Staple house wrap out of the way while you are installing the window.

3. Apply a generous amount of caulk (roughly $1/2$ inch) to sides and top of the opening exterior. Never place caulk along the bottom of the opening so in case of water intrusion, it has somewhere to go.

4. Place the window into the opening. Install one screw, if necessary, to hold it in place.

5. Plumb the window by placing a level on one side and ensuring the bubble in the level is perfectly centered. Use shims as needed, adjusting them until the window is level. Check your fit on the inside to ensure equal drywall reveal on all sides.

6. Open and close the window to make sure it operates properly.

7. Once you are certain your window is centered and plumb, use an impact driver to install a screw into all remaining holes of your window flange.

8. Once the window is installed, perform a final inspection by ensuring it raises and lowers easily.

9. Trim your shims so they are flush with the window jamb.

10. Use 4-inch window tape and install on left, right, and finally the top of the window. Once tape is installed on top, pull house wrap down over it.
11. Take seam tape and tape two corners of house wrap down.

SEVENTEEN

FLOORING

A smooth flooring install begins long before you lay that first piece of tile or wood. Producing a flat, level floor begins with your foundation. If you're building on a pier-and-beam foundation, taking your time installing the flooring system is important. Use a level and a string line to ensure every joist is as level as possible.

This was the point in our build when we began to feel hopeless. It was just us, spending twelve-hour days and moving what felt like only a few feet per day. Noell felt frustrated at the progress, but because Daniel had been in the flooring industry for so many years, he knew how important it was to get the flooring system level. His patience paid off: when it came time to install our floors, it was a breeze.

> Noell felt frustrated at the progress, but because Daniel had been in the flooring industry for so many years, he knew how important it was to get the flooring system level.

If you're building on a slab, make sure to let your concrete cure for at least thirty days, properly repairing any cracks that may occur. If there seems to be an issue with cracking, it might be necessary to install a crack isolation membrane coupled with self-leveling. If you notice heavy cracking (more than $1/4$ to $1/2$ inch), there may be underlying foundation issues that must be addressed before you begin installing your flooring.

SPECIFICATIONS

Manufacturers' specifications are incredibly important. *Always* take the time to read them before your install. It's not only important to know the recommended method of install, but it's imperative to follow it for warranty purposes. If there is ever an issue with your flooring (for example, cracks, cupping, or discoloration), the first question from the manufacturer will be: *Did you follow our guidelines?* All claims of defect will be rigorously investigated, and the last thing you want to do is give them a reason to deny your claim.

SUBSTRATES

A substrate is the surface that you'll be installing your flooring over. The question is: What type of flooring can be installed over top of what type of substrate?

Engineered wood floors, for example, can be installed over either a slab (with a moisture-barrier glue) or a subfloor (most commonly by nailing it, but some can be glued or floated).

Tile, however, must be installed over some type of concrete substrate, whether it be a concrete slab or a concrete board such as Hardie backer board or PermaBASE cement board. These products are most commonly glued and screwed/nailed to your subfloor. Mortar may stick (temporarily) to plywood, but it will not permanently bond.

> This is disastrous. . . . It will sound as though you are walking through a forest of cornflakes when walking across your floor.

Over the years, we have seen many remodels gone wrong. Too many people install tile directly over a wooden subfloor. This is disastrous, mainly due to the wood constantly expanding and contracting, which will cause mortar to release its bond and begin to crack. This will inevitably result in the shifting of tile and cracking of grout joints. It will sound as though you are walking through a forest of cornflakes when walking across your floor.

When redoing flooring, all of the following information in this chapter is important, but it is especially important to carefully follow the correct steps and ensure each step is done appropriately.

FLOOR PREP

Do you see the recurring theme here? Laying a sturdy foundation is the most important aspect of your build. The lack of proper steps prior to install of any product can be catastrophic, and it's no different with flooring. The use of self-leveler is a must (unless you're installing carpet, but still not a bad idea). Whether your house is one year old or a hundred, there is no substrate that is perfectly flat.

For example, if you were to put a transit level on your floor at one end of your slab, and then measure at the other end, they could be off by as much as a few inches. That doesn't mean you'll need to pour enough self-leveler to bring your entire floor up that high. Your goal is to reduce high and low spots within a certain area.

A 6- to 8-foot straight edge is a great tool to help with those elevation changes. We've seen some jobs that when you laid an 8-foot straight edge on the floor, there was as much as a 2-inch gap within that 8-foot span. Can you imagine trying to lay tile on that floor? From one end to the other, the straight edge was actually level, but the real key is to make your floor *flat*. Use these straight edges/levels to help you identify the high and low areas and then circle them. You can then go back and address them as necessary, whether it's to grind them down if too high or fill with self-leveler if low.

> Over the years, we have seen many remodels gone wrong.

When using a leveler, be sure to use proper primer and allow adequate dry time as recommended by the manufacturer. Once your leveler is dry, go back over it with a floor scraper. There will be small areas where bubbles and potential high spots occur. Use a 4- or 6-inch scraper to knock down these areas. Sweep and vacuum all areas thoroughly. Now you're ready to start laying out your floor.

LAYOUT

Now that your floor is flat, clean, and ready to go, where do you start? Which orientation should you run your wood or tile floors? What pattern does your product follow? For the most part, there are no definite answers to these questions, only suggestions.

For example, wood floors are typically oriented vertically or in line with your front door. This elongates the area, which gives the room a more open, spacious feel. However, there are some cases where the

foyer wall stops abruptly after the front door, and it makes more sense to orient the flooring horizontally or left to right of the front door.

Another tip is to run your flooring "with the light." Starting at your front door, which direction does the main source of natural light come from? Install your floors in line with that natural light.

Here are some basic steps to get started:

1. Once you've determined your layout, it's time to start measuring. The first thing that you'll need to do is square up your room. We do this by using a 3–4–5 method also known as a Pythagorean triple. Remember your ninth-grade geometry class? We're going to use this to complete the task.

2. Start with your longest exterior wall. The reason is that this wall should hypothetically be the most square. Assuming the flooring material you chose is 12 inches wide, place a mark 12 inches away from the wall at one end of the wall and then another mark 12 inches away from the wall at the other end. Use a chalk line to snap a line between the two points. Now go to the adjacent wall and place another mark at 12 inches on one end and 12 inches on the other. Using your chalk line, snap another line between those two points. From the point where your two lines cross, place a mark 4 feet down the longest line. Then again, from the point where the two lines cross, place a mark 3 feet down the shortest line. If the room is square, the distance between your two marks will be exactly 5 feet. This method is heavily used throughout the framing of your home. For larger areas, you can also use the 6-8-10 method, which is the same but with larger integers.

3. Now that our room is square, we can finally start laying our floors.

WOOD FLOORS

The use of wood flooring as a finished floor dates back to the early nineteenth century. Although the overall appearance of the floor covering is different today, it's still a popular option to create a timeless look for your home.

There are various types of tongue-and-groove wood flooring products to choose from, and the method of installation will rely mostly on the product you choose. Besides being tongue and groove, the one major difference between wood and tile installation is that wood floors require the installation of a moisture barrier. Wood does not mix well with moisture. Therefore, necessary precautions must take place before installation. Thoroughly read the manufacturer's specifications to ensure proper install.

Before reading the instructions, you'll need to identify what type of substrate you have. Manufacturers will list their specifications per each type of substrate. If you have a wood substrate, most times they will simply call for the installation of a 6 mil layer of plastic or tar paper before install. Read the instructions carefully, as there may be specs that are required to maintain your warranty.

MOISTURE LEVELS

There are several different ways to test your slab moisture levels: the relative humidity test, the calcium chloride test, the "plastic sheet method," and the use of a moisture meter probe, which is the most popular method of testing. You can buy a decent probe for around a hundred dollars, which will be money well spent. It could save you from spending thousands on removal and replacement of damaged flooring. Be sure to test multiple locations of the proposed area, paying close attention to the areas near windows and doors.

Also, it's a good idea to map the area, documenting the levels in each spot, complete with pictures and written records. This way, if there's ever a warranty issue, you'll have some proof that moisture levels were within the approved tolerance range. The National Wood Flooring Association (NWFA) states that concrete slabs are required to be below 75 percent relative humidity for proper installation to occur. There are wood flooring adhesives that can be used to combat higher moisture levels, but again, read the instructions to determine the maximum level of moisture they recommend installing their product over.

> *Tip:* To determine how much flooring material you will need: First, multiply the length of your space times the width of your space. Then multiply this total by 8–10 percent to account for waste. Add these two numbers together for the total square footage you will need.

TYPES OF WOOD FLOORS

Now that your slab is prepped, and you have ensured that the substrate's moisture levels are acceptable, let's talk about the different types of wood floors you can install.

There are three main methods to install wood flooring.

Nail Down

The most expensive option is the nail-down sand and stain wood floor. Think of your granny's wood floors; they were solid wood stained to perfection and probably a hundred years old. In the South, many of these floors were made of heart pine and as gorgeous and resilient as they come. Heart pine was used because it has a tight grain and is durable. This type of floor is purchased in raw tongue-and-groove form and requires many steps to complete the install. It must be acclimated to its end environment for a minimum of two to three weeks. This ensures that the moisture levels in the product are within 2–4 percent of the subfloor per the NWFA.

If you have a concrete substrate, you must install a plywood subfloor to have something to nail your wood flooring to. Before installation, the approved moisture barrier must be installed. Once nailed down, the wood gets sanded, stained, and three layers of polyurethane applied. As you can see, this process is laborious and requires someone of great knowledge and talent to complete the task. If this is the type of floor you want, it will require a lot of time and research to tackle this as a DIY.

Glue Down

Engineered wood flooring is a unique type of flooring in that some manufacturers specify that it can be nailed down, glued down, or floated—making it the most versatile of the bunch. Many people in our region of the country choose an engineered wood floor (which is most commonly a glue-down application), simply because Florida homes are predominantly built on concrete slabs. Engineered wood flooring has a layered plywood base and a hardwood veneer on top as the finished product. The plywood base is more water resistant, which helps reduce potential issues caused by moisture such as cupping, warping, and discoloration. However, it's still imperative to ensure that moisture levels in the proposed area of installation are within the tolerance of the product prior to install. In our area, we've seen and heard all too often of moisture issues arising after installation.

Floating

The last type of flooring installation is floating. This means that the floor is not adhered to the substrate in any way. The weight of the product holds the floor in place, and the base molding or shoe molding holds down the edges. The most common floated flooring is luxury vinyl plank (LVP). LVP has made a big name for itself over the past five to eight years. The fact that it is waterproof is the biggest attraction given that its predecessor, laminate flooring, was not. LVP is also very durable and is scratch resistant. Another benefit to LVP is that most manufacturers include a soft backing attached to the product.

This does two things:

Floating wood floor

1. It reduces noise.
2. It allows slight "give" or cushion when walked on. Given its cushion, this product is highly recommended for people with knee or back pain and is the preferable option over tile, which has no cushion.

TILE FLOORS

As we've stated many times: function first, aesthetics second. Scrubbing grout lines is not a fun chore, so choosing larger tiles that give you smaller grout lines will save you many hours of headache in the future. On a side note, the easiest way to get your grout clean is to hire someone to come in and steam clean it.

Choosing Tile

Like anything, there's a range of options depending on your budget. Here's an overview:

Least expensive. Floor & Décor is one of the cheapest places to get tile; just do not be afraid to be picky. Buy more than you need, and carefully go through each box, choosing the best pieces from each and returning the rest.

Middle grade. Some high-end brands have put out more affordable lines that make their impeccable designs more attainable. We used the Jeffrey Court Home Depot line throughout our home and were very impressed with the quality.

High end. Places like TileBar or Jeffery Court produce unique, high-end tile if you want to splurge.

Types of Tiles

There are more types of tiles than you might imagine. These listed here are the most popular and are our favorite go-to tiles. Research each to see which best serves your budget and style preferences.

Ceramic tile. This is the most affordable tile option and is the perfect choice for any installation if it is not in contact with water for prolonged periods of time—basically, anything but a tub or shower surround. Unglazed ceramic will give you a more rustic finish, while glazed ceramic will provide more protection to ensure your floor stands the test of time.

Porcelain tile. After ceramic, porcelain is the next most popular and affordable option. You can find porcelain tile in many colors, shapes, and styles, making it a very versatile option.

Glass tile. These tiles are a little more expensive and can be very fragile, though very stain resistant. This makes them the perfect choice for a backsplash or shower inlay and band.

Cement tile. We have seen a recent resurgence for cement tiles, though they date back to the nineteenth century. They offer some very beautiful designs and colors, though they require monthly resealing to maintain their beauty. It's certainly not the most affordable or low-maintenance option, but it can be great in a low-traffic area.

Mosaic tile. Mosaics can be very pricey, but if you use them in areas where small quantities are needed like bands, inlays, or shower floors, you can add visual interest without breaking your budget. (Side note: this is the best tile choice for your shower floor as it allows you to easily create the fall needed to move your water to the drain.)

Natural tile. We would strongly caution anyone attempting a tile install for the first time to stay away from a natural stone such as marble or travertine. There is no margin for error, as many of them are butt jointed without the forgiveness of a wider grout line. These products are more expensive, higher maintenance, and more susceptible to damage.

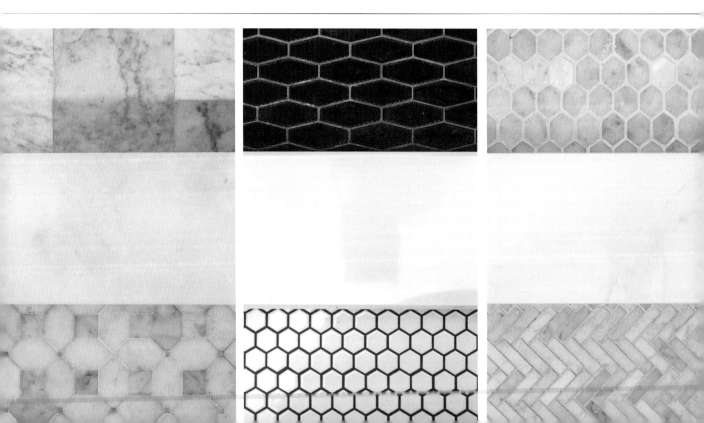

Tile Installation

The installation of tile can be a daunting task, and to be clear, it's not for the faint of heart. However, with the correct tools and a few tips, you can be on your way to saving some serious cash. If you're anything like us, you'll want to know all potential hazards before jumping into the water.

In recent years, plank tile ranging anywhere from 6×24 to 12×72 has become a main flooring trend in the industry. It has thin grout lines and offers a lovely wood look but has the durability of tile. However, installation of this product proves very difficult compared to a square tile.

The presence of "lippage" or "toe kicks" after install is a *huge* issue in the industry with these tiles. Part of the difficulty of install is created in the manufacturing itself. Most plank tiles have a slight bow to them. For some reason, the product tends to cup or curl during the drying phase of production. Think of it like this: Now you have an imperfect slab, with an imperfect product, and it is your job to make the tiles perfectly flat. How is that even possible?

The manufacturer's solution is to require a certain pattern (one-third lap), which means every third row of tiles should line up. This helps to evenly distribute the curvature of the tile, reducing the potential "lippage." But without the use of self-leveler and maybe even leveling clips, it's still an uphill battle. We would not recommend attempting a plank tile install without the use of leveling clips.

Staying Square

We've already addressed a few hazards with lippage and leveling. The other major problem that people encounter when installing tile is getting off square. The slightest twist in a couple of tiles can cause you to veer off course on a swift road to disaster. Some people rely fully on spacers to mitigate this problem. We steer away from this method because all tiles are not the same size, and although spacers and leveling clips have come a long way, how do we know every spacer or clip will be either?

The easiest way to ensure this doesn't occur is to map out a grid or "snap lines" of your tile layout throughout the entire proposed area. Depending on the size of the tile (and how far you're willing to stretch during install), you may choose to map your grid to include two rows (four tiles per square). This grid doesn't necessarily have to include every tile. You can map out more rows for smaller tiles or less for larger tiles. For example, if your tile measurement (including grout lines) of two tiles is 24 inches, then you'll have a grid that's 24×24.

Where do you start your grid? Remember the lines you snapped to ensure that the room was square? Those two lines will serve as your control lines and will be the point of origin where you will begin measuring from. Start from one side of your control line (the longest line that was snapped previously with your chalk box) and measure out two rows of tile (including grout joints).

Basic Tools for Installing Tile

When installing tile, you'll need a few basic tools to create an easy, successful project.

Wet saw. Wet saws are great for cutting tile, but the problem is they use water, and overspray can be an issue. For this reason, most of the time the wet saw must be set up outside. What does that mean for you? When you need a cut, you must stop, get up off the floor, walk outside, make your cut, walk back inside, get back down on your knees, and then install your cut. The slide cutter works by scoring your tile and then snapping it in two pieces right there beside you. No standing up, no walking outside, no walking back inside. Simply score and snap. This is a huge time-saver. The purchase of a decent quality cutter is well worth the money in time saved. Plus, you can keep it for other projects to come.

Slide cutter. As mentioned earlier, this extremely helpful tool saves not only time but your back and knees as well. The slide cutter is made up of basic components such as a rail, handle, base, and tiny cutting wheel no bigger than a shirt button.

Margin trowel. This essential tool can be used for a multitude of things while installing—most commonly to help lift a tile once it has been laid. Sometimes the need will arise to apply more material below a tile, and this tool will greatly assist in doing so.

Trowel. Used correctly, a trowel applies the exact amount of mortar every time you spread it. Be sure to use the correct-sized notch trowel for your install. For example, if your tile is a mosaic tile on a sheet, you don't want to use anything larger than a $3/16$-inch-by-$3/16$-inch notch trowel because your thin-set will squeeze through the joints, creating a huge mess. If you're installing plank tile or anything that is larger than 18×18 tile, you will need to use a $1/2$-inch-by-$1/2$-inch square notch trowel. This size will apply a larger amount of thin-set, thus giving more "float" room to make adjustments.

Leveling clips. Leveling clip systems are abundant these days and have been on the market for the better portion of ten years, give or take. These systems have progressively gotten better and easier to use over the years. Used correctly, they can turn any novice into a capable tile setter very quickly. They can be pricey and will slow you down a bit until you get accustomed to them, but the overall cost benefit is well worth it. We highly recommend the use of leveling clips for most tile applications.

Grouting Tools and Tips

Following are a few key tools that will help you with the grouting process:

- **At least five 5-gallon buckets:** Three buckets should be a little more than halfway full of clean water (half full prevents water from spilling). One bucket will be for mixing, and one bucket will be for cleaning your mixer. Also, the use of bucket dollies isn't a necessity, but it will save your back from a lot of strain.
- **A fresh pack of sponges:** These can be purchased at any major hardware store in packs of three or five.
- **Drill:** A ½-inch corded spade handle drill with a mixing paddle bit (the same drill used to mix your thin-set) will be needed. This drill size is necessary because of the torque required to mix the product.
- **A grout float:** This tool is what you will use to spread your grout into the joints.

Now that you have all the proper tools, here are some pointers to make the job a little easier and produce better results:

1. Do *not* mix your grout with hot water. This will speed up the chemical reaction and cause your grout to set up quickly, thus making it harder to spread. In fact, some manufacturers recommend mixing your grout with ice water. This slows the curing process and gives you more time to spread and clear wipe. The next tip is to mix your grout with distilled water.
2. Pour a manageable amount of grout (covering approximately 300 to 400 square feet at a time) onto your tile and use your grout float to spread the grout into the joints.
3. Make sure to press your float firmly on the tile as you spread, and keep the angle of your float as close to 90 degrees as possible. The goal is to clean all the grout off the tile, only leaving it in the joints. It will help also to spread across your joints at a 45-degree angle in a sweeping "S" motion, never lifting your float off the tile.

TILE INSTALLATION

The benefits of using tile flooring far outweigh their cost, and that said, they can be quite inexpensive. Additionally, tile floors are durable, water resistant, eco-friendly, easy to clean, and add to your home's resale value.

Materials and tools needed:

thin-set
notch trowel (size is dependent on grout type)
tile (type and amounts vary depending on preference and space)
slide cutter or wet saw
leveling clips
margin trowel
bucket of distilled water
sponges
1/2-inch spade handle drill
mixing paddle
grout
grout float
4-inch grinder

Other tools as needed:

tape measure
knee pads
bucket dollies (optional)

Helpful steps for installing tile:

1. Spread thin-set with the correct size trowel onto the floor. Be sure to leave grid lines exposed so you can install each tile on the lines as you go. If using leveling clips, they will help you stay lined up as well as do their job, which is to keep every tile level with the next. (Note: Some people prefer to lay all their full tiles first and then go back and do all the cuts with a slide cutter later. This is just a personal preference, and you can choose however you would like, but both methods get the job done.)

2. Wipe any excess thin-set away from the tiles and joints as you go. If your joint is full of thin-set, you can use any small object that will slide between the tiles to dig it out. Usually your margin trowel will do the trick, but you can also use your pencil, a razor knife, or something similar.

3. Once you have a section done, be sure to block it off. If someone or something *does* walk on it, it's not the end of the world and the tiles can be removed and reset, but your goal is to move toward the finish line during your build, not to create unnecessary work for yourself.

4. Now that your tile has set up overnight and all leveling clips or spacers have been removed, it's time to mix the grout and apply using a grout float.

5. Once everything is grouted, wrap things up by "swirling" and "clear wiping." With a clean bucket of water by your side, use a sponge to

clean the excess grout off your tile in a swirling motion. Be careful not to dig your grout out of the joints, press lightly as you swirl, and rinse your sponge regularly.

6. Pay close attention to detail when swirling over top of the joints to ensure that the grout widths are consistent throughout.

7. When clear wiping, it is essential to use only clean water throughout the process. Rotate buckets as often as possible, and use only one pass of a fresh, clean sponge, wipe at a 45-degree angle, flip your sponge over, and pass only once again before rinsing. This process eliminates any haze or grout residue from the tile.

nail down

WOOD FLOORS

Besides having different methods of adhesion, or lack thereof, installation of any type of wood flooring is basically the same. Once you grasp the concepts required to install wood floors, you will easily be able to install any type. The most important thing is to ensure your first row stays exactly on your control line. The proper install of every other row will only be possible if the first row is done correctly.

Materials and tools needed:

flooring material of your choice (types and amounts vary depending on size of space and preference)
chalk line
hammer
tapping blocks
2-inch painter's tape

Other tools as needed:

knee pads
air compressor
air hose
pneumatic wood flooring nailer
rubber mallets
trowel
table, miter, and jigsaw
adhesive
wood floor cleats or staples
wood flooring strap clamps

Tip: When installing around entryways or walls, be sure to allow enough room for expansion and contraction of your floor. In most cases, 1/4 inch is adequate, but be mindful of base or door casing coverage.

Helpful steps for installing wood floors:

1. First, determine the orientation or direction the wood floor will run. The general rule of thumb is to run the floor perpendicular to the front door threshold—meaning front to back when you walk into the home.

2. If possible, start the first row on the longest exterior wall in the home. Much like tile, check the area for squareness, and using your chalk line, snap a control line as your guideline. Wood floors are installed in a staggered pattern and very few, if any, butt joints will line up throughout the room. We like to leave at least the width of each board between each butt joint. For example, if you have a 6-inch-wide plank, make sure to start your next butt joint 6 inches or farther away from the previous row's joint. Use a hammer and tapping block to ensure that all your joints are tight.

3. When using the glue-down method, use tape every few rows to keep the joints tight. A time-saving pro tip is to overlap your tape on the previous section. This way, when the glue is dry, you can easily remove each row of the tape from your starting point in one pull.

EIGHTEEN

MOLDINGS

M oldings are used throughout homes to not only create a more seamless look by hiding joints, seams, imperfections, or gaps between walls, the floor, and the ceiling but also to add dimension, definition, style, and character. Molding can also be used to make a space feel cozier and soften transitions between things like a floor and a wall. It's important to choose moldings that fit the style you're trying to create in your home. You don't want to choose Victorian-style moldings in a modern-style home. It's perfectly fine to mix or match molding styles as long as they have similar lines.

TYPES OF MOLDING

There are three main types of molding:

- **Crown molding.** Crown molding adds such a finished look to your space. There are many designs to choose from, but choosing one with several pieces that build up to the look you are going for versus just one large piece will be more affordable and easier to install. Choosing crown molding that takes up more wall space than ceiling space will make your space feel bigger, whereas crown molding that takes up more ceiling space than wall space will help create a cozier feel if you have high ceilings.

- **Baseboards.** Baseboards can be as simple as traditional with straight edges, a few-piece pattern, or intricately carved designs. The guidelines listed below are flexible, so choose whatever style you think best fits your home, keeping in mind the following guidelines for baseboard heights and noting the taller your baseboard is, the smaller your room will appear.
  - Eight-foot ceilings: 3^1/$_2$–5 inches
  - Nine-foot ceilings: 5–7 inches
  - Ten-foot-plus ceilings: 6–10 inches
- **Casings.** Casings are the moldings that go around the doors and windows in the interior of your home. Dressing up your doors and windows with casings adds so much character to your home—in our opinion, they set the tone for the room.

MOLDING MATERIALS AND TIPS

Molding is typically made of one of the following three options:

- **Medium-density fiberboard:** Medium-density fiberboard (MDF) is formed from sawdust and resin, is the least expensive option, and is easy to paint. However, it's not easy to repair if damaged and easily swells if exposed to water, so it's not the best for use in moisture-prone areas.
- **Finger-jointed pine:** Pine is moderately priced and perhaps the best wood option for painting. It can be repaired if damaged and can also be purchased already primed, saving you a step.
- **Hardwood:** This is the best option for staining and can be easily repaired. It's also the most expensive of the three.

HOW TO MEASURE FOR MOLDINGS

Measure the total linear length of your wall for crown and base and all sides of your doors and windows. Add up each of these totals and add an extra 25 percent to accommodate for waste. Most moldings come in 8-, 12-, or 16-foot pieces. Try to purchase the lengths that will allow you to cover the entire wall in one piece if possible, as seams can be difficult and unsightly.

PAINTING MOLDINGS

Before you paint, it's vital to fill all nail holes with filler or putty. Allow to dry, then gently rub with sandpaper to make them smooth. Caulk is so important in molding installation; it can make all your mistakes virtually disappear. Even if your cuts are not exact, caulk will smooth them out, and once painted, no one will be the wiser.

Tips for cutting molding:

Inside corners:

To cut the left side of an inside corner, miter-cut with the saw blade rotated right at 45 degrees and use the right side of the cut. To cut the right side of an inside corner, rotate the saw blade left at 45 degrees and use the left side of the cut.

Outside corners:

To cut the left side of an outside corner, rotate the saw blade right at 45 degrees and use the right side of the cut. To cut the right side of the corner, rotate the saw blade left at 45 degrees and use the left side.

Scarf joint:

Rather than just butting two straight pieces together with square cuts, use a scarf joint to make the joint look more seamless. Cut the one piece as though it were a left inside corner and the other as if it were a right side of an outside corner. They will now fit neatly together.

Molding can be purchased already primed, but if yours is not, it's easier to prime everything and let dry for at least an hour before installing. You can also go ahead and paint it, but you may still need to do a touch-up coat once it is installed. If you decide to paint the moldings in place, put painter's tape along the top and bottom of the moldings where they meet the wall and ceiling.

Caulk is so important in molding installation; it can make all your mistakes virtually disappear.

Project:

MOLDING INSTALLATION

One of the most important pieces of advice in construction (and in life) rings *especially* true in moldings: "Measure twice, cut once!" Ensuring you have exact measurements and precise cuts will make installing moldings so much easier. Taking the time to ensure the lengths and angles are perfect before you lower that saw blade will save you a lot of headaches.

Materials and tools needed:

tape measure
pencil and paper
stud finder
crown molding of your choice
12-inch sliding miter saw
16- or 18-gauge finish nailer
hammer
nail punch
wood filler or putty
caulk gun
paintable caulk
paint
wood glue

Other materials as needed:

level
1- to 2-inch finish nails
air compressor
air hose
table saw
circular saw
speed square
carpenter's wood glue
shims
sandpaper
ladders

Helpful steps for installing crown molding:

1. Carefully measure each wall from corner to corner. Write down all measurements.
2. Use a stud finder to locate the studs throughout the room, and mark them a few inches down from where the wall and ceiling meet using a light pencil. This will serve as a guide so that you'll know where to place nails.
3. Cut crown molding pieces with visible decorative surface up, positioned at a 45-degree angle on the miter saw table. The top of the crown molding sits against the vertical back fence of the saw, and the bottom edge is against the vertical back fence of the saw.
4. Begin install with the wall opposite the door you enter. Put crown into position, making sure it forms the appropriate angle against the wall and ceiling. If it has a flat space on the top and bottom, make sure it fits flush against the wall and ceiling. If you are using a crown design that has several pieces, begin installing the top one first, then add in your other pieces.
5. Once you are certain your angle is correct, use your nail gun to secure your moldings, making sure you nail where the studs are.
6. After all moldings are nailed into place, use a hammer and a nail punch to drive any nails that are sticking up down into the wood.
7. Use wood filler or putty to fill nail holes and fill seams with caulk.
8. Now it's time to paint.

Note: When installing crown molding, you will need to understand the difference between a miter and a bevel. To set a miter cut to a specific angle, you must use the horizontal adjustment on your saw. And for a bevel cut, use the vertical adjustment. Crown molding installation requires the exact, correct combination of the two. The easiest way to achieve the correct combination is through online searches. There are many sources online that will provide you with accurate angle chart information on crown molding.

Helpful steps for installing baseboard:

1. Use a stud finder to mark studs several inches above the floor to serve as a guide for your nailing pattern.
2. Measure each wall where you intend to install baseboards and compile a cut list of these measurements. This will save you time by eliminating one-by-one measuring and cutting. If you have cuts in the middle of the wall, use a scarf joint. For outside corners, cut ends at 90 degrees; for inside corners, cut ends at 45 degrees.
3. Butt your baseboards into door casings using a 90-degree cut. Once cuts are made and you have dry-fit your boards to ensure everything fits perfectly, nail baseboards into studs when possible or roughly 8–10 inches apart using a finish nailer.
4. Once all boards are attached, use a nail punch to drive in any nails sticking out, then fill in all holes using putty or filler.
5. Caulk all joints, let dry, then paint.

Helpful steps for installing casing:

1. First, measure and draw a "reveal line" about ¼ inch from the inner part of the door frame to serve as your guide for installing the inside edge of the casing. Make sure this line is the same distance from the frame on both sides and the top of the door.
2. Attach any decorative blocks or rosettes to the wall first with the nail gun.

Helpful steps for installing mitered casing:

1. Hold the head casing piece in place, then mark it with a small pencil mark where the top reveal line crosses the side reveal lines.
2. Use the miter saw to cut a 45-degree angle on this mark.

3. With an 18-gauge nail gun, install the head casing in place, making sure the longer edge is on top. Attach the inside portion to the door frame using 1-inch finish nails, and attach the thicker outside edge using 2-inch nails.

Helpful steps for installing side casing:

1. Place these pieces against the installed head casing, making a mark where the inside corner of the head casing meets the inside of the side casing boards.
2. Cut a 45-degree angle on this mark that will allow the side casings to fit perfectly into the head casing.
3. Use wood glue to attach the edges of the side and head pieces together, then nail the side pieces in place. Use a damp cloth to wipe away any excess glue.

Helpful steps for installing butted casing:

1. Measure and cut your side pieces and nail into place on your reveal line.
2. Line up the head casing pieces level with your reveal line on top of the door frame and nail into place. If you have several pieces in your pattern, work from the bottom piece up.

NINETEEN

LIGHTING DESIGN

Who doesn't love that elegant, Parisian-café look of string lights carelessly strung across the ceiling? We get ours at Costco inexpensively, and the nice thing about string lights is that you can opt for either plug-in or solar powered. So, if you don't have an outlet accessible, you can simply use the solar-powered string lights and attach them to the side of the house.

Or, if you have the builder-grade exterior lights, you can replace them with gorgeous hanging lights that make a statement. World Market is a great place to search for those, but we've found them even cheaper at T.J. Maxx and Marshalls.

Adding statement and string lights is one way to both brighten up and elevate a space.

> Adding statement and string lights is one way to both brighten up and elevate a space.

STAGES OF LIGHTING

Lighting is such an integral part of your build that it can literally make or break your design, though many people don't put much budget or thought toward it. Of course, our favorite is natural lighting, but that step is covered during the beginning stages of your home design.

Now it's time to design a lighting plan that's functional and beautiful. Laying out your lighting plan must be done early on to ensure proper wiring to incorporate the fixtures and features you desire without anything having to be rewired or changed, causing an increase in costs. Carefully think through every room and write down the following:

- How will this space be used? Will your dining room table also be used to do homework with your kids? Will your living room be used for reading? Try to really think through any possible activity that will take place in each room.
- What time of day will each space be used?
- What type and how much natural lighting will each space receive?
- Are there architectural pieces, artwork, built-ins, fireplaces, or anything you want to draw attention to?

TYPES OF LIGHTING

Before you begin designing your plan, understand there are three different types of lighting:

Ambient: Ambient lighting provides even, overall lighting to a space. Full ambient lighting is attained by perfectly spaced recessed lights. Ambient lighting includes recessed lighting, pendants, and chandeliers.

Task: Task lighting illuminates areas where your daily activities, such as cooking, doing homework, or getting ready, take place. Sources of task lighting include track, recessed, or table and floor lamps. In the kitchen, pendants and under-cabinet lighting provide plenty of light for food prep and cooking.

Accent: Accent lighting is the first layer to be considered in an area such as a hallway. It's used to draw attention to desired items such as art, plants, a walkway, bookcases, trees, or water features. This type of lighting includes chandeliers, pendants, and sconces.

TYPES OF LIGHTING FIXTURES

Just as the quality of light can really set the mood for a room, the fixture itself can too. Half of the day, main lighting is often not turned on, but the fixture is always there. This piece is often overlooked during a remodel, especially for a built-in overhead light fixture. Think about it—you don't want to spend all this time and money updating a room and leave a dated fixture to detract from all your hard work.

Be sure to select fixtures that match or blend well with your chosen architectural styles (see chapter 5).

DESIGN YOUR LIGHTING PLAN

Now it's time to design your lighting plan. Here are some basic steps to get you started:

1. Set your budget. Look at your overall budget and determine how much you can allocate toward lighting. There are light fixtures for all budgets, but you need to know what exactly you are working with so you can create a plan that properly illuminates your home without breaking the bank.

2. If you find a stunning light fixture you love but it is out of your price range, do some research. There are many affordable lighting options out there. We sourced almost all our focal-point lighting from Capitol Lighting because they offer various styles for all budgets and have great sales, great customer service, and are a family-owned business. But we saved money by mixing in low-budget lighting from places like IKEA, Amazon.com, World Market, and Target and putting it in places that were not as noticeable. You can seamlessly blend a $5,000 chandelier with $25 gooseneck lights, and no one will be the wiser.

3. Set the mood. If you haven't already, create a Pinterest or mood board with the type of lighting you would like to see in each room. This will help you decide on a theme and narrow down your design type.

4. Begin your design. Start with your ambient lighting and work backward from there.

5. Decide if each room will contain a chandelier-style or pendant. There's nothing worse than getting a chandelier you love so much into your home and realizing it's not going to fit where you envisioned it. This happened with the chandelier that now hangs in our stairwell. It was originally intended for over our bed, but due to some confusion about its actual dimensions listed online, it basically would have been touching our bed hanging from our 10-foot ceiling.

Thankfully, it worked perfectly in our stairwell, and we still get to enjoy its beauty. If you purchase lighting online, make sure to determine whether it will work in your space before you install it. Once the wires are cut, it's no longer returnable, and you will be the proud owner of a light that does not work for you and less money in your budget than you expected.

6. Lay out your recessed lighting during this step. Recessed lighting should be equally spaced across the ceiling and aligned in a grid determined by the shape of the room.

7. Take it to task. Now that you have designed your ambient lighting, you can begin choosing your task lighting. Determine the tasks you will be doing in each room and what kind of lighting you will need to complete them. This can include under-cabinet lighting in your kitchen, desk lamps for reading, or vanity lights for grooming.

8. Choose your accent. Do you have any artwork, furniture, or architectural details you want to highlight? For example, we wanted to highlight the leaded glass transom in our foyer. Using eyeball or 2- to 4-inch recessed lighting is perfect for this application.

9. Determine your light switch placement. Think through how you will enter and exit each room at different times of the day. Giving this careful consideration will allow you to easily light your home when you come out of your bedroom in the morning and when you arrive home after dark. You don't want to have to walk all the way to the front of the house on your way into the bedroom at night, and you don't want to have to walk through a dark house to turn on lights.

Put as many lights as desired on a dimmer switch; this will allow you to fully control the amount of light in each room. Dimmers are great on all ambient lighting; at minimum, we recommend them in your dining room and owner's bedroom and bathroom, especially if you have a soaking tub.

GUIDELINES FOR LIGHTING

The following are all standard recommendations but not steadfast rules. Feel free to adjust as needed to fit your home and your family's needs.

Height of chandelier or pendant. Have 2 to 3 inches of height for every foot of ceiling height. A room with a 15-foot ceiling could easily have a 30- to 45-inch chandelier.

Height from floor. This should not be closer than 7 feet from the floor. In a two-story space, the light should hang level with the second floor, and in the foyer, at least 6 inches above the door.

Diameter of a chandelier. Add the length and the width of the room together. This number, in inches, will give you the proper diameter for a chandelier light fixture. For example, in a living room that is 15 feet by 20 feet in size, the total is 35 feet. In this situation, a 35-inch-diameter light fixture would be the best fit.

Pendants over kitchen island. To determine the appropriate size of pendants for above your island, take the width of your island countertop in feet and add it to the length of your countertop in feet. That number in inches is the ideal width for your pendant lighting. For example, if your island is 5 feet wide and 10 feet long, you would look for pendants that are approximately 15 inches wide. Determining the distance between your pendants is the easiest decision to make as it is a standard 18 inches between your pendants and 18 inches between the light and the edge of the island. Also, the typical rule is to allow 30 to 36 inches between your countertop and the bottom of your chandelier, but feel free to adjust as needed.

While determining how many pendants you want over your island is largely a personal choice, there are some guidelines to help you with your decision:

Small island: Anything under 5 feet by 2 to 3 feet would look best with only two pendants.

Medium island: Anything 5 to 10 feet by 4 feet will look great with two or three pendants. If you choose to go with two, that will allow you to go a little bit larger than the previously mentioned guideline.

Large island: Anything 10 feet by 4 feet or over will look great with at least three pendants.

- **Dining room.** Above your table, choose a fixture that is at least 1 foot shorter than the total length of the table. When you hang it, leave a space between 28 and 36 inches from the bottom of the fixture to the tabletop. Avoid downlights as much as possible in this room to avoid shadows on faces. If possible, this is the perfect room to include eye-level lights on the walls.

- **Bathroom lighting.** Bathroom sconces should be placed at eye level on either side of the mirror, approximately 65 inches from the floor. Lights over the mirror should be placed anywhere from 75 to 80 inches from the floor. Over a bathtub, you want the bottom of the light at least 8 feet from the top of the tub.

Project:

INSTALLING A LIGHTING FIXTURE

Although many people find the thought of installing or changing a light fixture intimidating, as no one wants to find themselves on the receiving end of a jolt of electricity, it's actually not nearly as difficult as many fear it is.

Materials and tools needed:

voltage tester pen
cordless drill
light fixture
wire nuts
ladder (optional, if needed)

Tip: Remember that the black wire is your hot, or live, wire, white is your neutral wire, and the copper or green wire is your ground wire.

Helpful steps for installing wall-mounted lighting:

1. Turn off the breaker that controls the circuit you will be working on.
2. If you are working on a remodel, detach and pull out the existing fixture to expose wires.
3. Using a voltage tester pen, touch the hot wire, which will be black. If the power is still on, your pen will beep—meaning you have the wrong circuit turned off. Repeat until you verify the power is off.
4. For a remodel, remove wire nuts on the neutral wire, which is white; the hot wire, which is black; and the ground wire, which is green or bare copper. If you are working at a new construction job, you will need to strip back about a quarter inch of sheathing on each wire to expose the copper wire.
5. With a cordless drill, install the mounting bracket of the new fixture.
6. Twist the ends of the white wire in the electrical box and the white wire in the light fixture together in a clockwise direction, and secure them with a wire nut, also screwed on clockwise.
7. Next, twist the ends of the black wires together in a clockwise direction, and secure with a wire nut.
8. Connect the ground wire from the electrical box to the fixture's ground wire, and secure with a wire nut.
9. Once all wires are secured, it's a good idea to make sure the fixture works. To do so, add a light bulb, turn the breaker back on, and flip the light switch to the "on" position.

10. Once operation is verified, *turn the breaker back off*. Then tuck all wires behind the mounting bracket of the fixture.

11. Place the fixture over the bolts protruding from the mounting bracket, and rotate it until the bolts slip through the keyholes of the fixture.

12. Using the manufacturer-provided nuts, twist onto the bolts until the fixture is secure in place.

13. Screw in any remaining light bulbs, turn the breaker back on, and double-check operation of the fixture.

TWENTY

OUTDOOR SPACES

T hough never in a million years would we have thought to put a pond in our yard, once we had one—thanks to The Pond Guy, Greg Wittstock—it quickly became our favorite place to spend time, especially for Daniel. We love entertaining there, whether in the daytime, just listening to the waterfall, or building a bonfire at night.

To create an outdoor space you love on a budget, either DIY some furniture using pallets or find used pieces you can freshen up. Noell once secured outdoor Pottery Barn chairs for less than $100, and another time she found an outdoor sectional sitting on the side of the road. She ordered new cushions from Target and had a beautiful new outdoor sofa. Add some tables where you can set drinks and prop your feet up with a good book. Pick up a few outdoor pillows from Marshalls, add some solar-powered outdoor lights (depending on how far your seating area is from electrical outlets) and some simple white candles, and you have a cozy entertaining area. Though the space is already outdoors, we still love pulling in live plants to tie the space back into nature, and bonus points if you are surrounded by trees—free decor.

PLANTERS

Planters are an incredibly easy way to create boundaries and define spaces in your backyard or patio space. You can opt for low-maintenance plants like ferns, ivy, succulents, and evergreen vines. Or if you

have a green thumb and like to change things up for the seasons, you can plant hydrangeas in the spring, mums in the fall, sunflowers in the winter, or whatever works for your climate and your area. You can find affordable oversized planters at Goodwill, and then add spray paint or "mud" to make them your desired color.

PORCHES

The first item on Noell's nonnegotiable list was a wraparound porch. Some of her favorite memories from childhood were swinging the afternoon away on the porch of her grandmother's Victorian home, lemonade in one hand and the latest copy of *Country Living* in the other. She always knew that when she grew up, she wanted a home with a beautiful porch.

Now that we have one, it's the first space Noell updates each season or holiday. It's the perfect way to give homes a perennial refresh without having to spend lots of money, and it keeps homes feeling fresh and new. Each season, simply clear out everything, throw it in a bin dedicated to the season, and store it until the following year.

DRAPERIES

For an elegant look, add draperies around the perimeter of your porch. This can be as simple and inexpensive as drop cloths. Daniel's mom's parents have a gazebo out by the river, and we went in with a few inexpensive PVC poles and brackets, and hung drop cloths from them, which instantly added more whimsy. Get the drop cloths at any home improvement store, such as Lowe's or Home Depot, and then sew a simple line across the top to put the pole through, or attach hanging clips to the fabric itself. IKEA is also a great place to buy curtains for this, if you prefer curtains over drop cloths.

Create a more rustic look with a darker drop cloth or dress it up with creamy sheers.

PAINT

Paint is the cheapest way to upgrade anything. Just grab a gallon of paint, and you can cover the floor, the ceiling, and the trim in a fresh coat and give your home instant gloss. Sky blue is an airy and gorgeous look for ceilings and is quick to be an eye-catcher, plus this color is said to keep birds and bugs from making your porch ceiling their home, meaning less work to keep it clean. You can paint a pattern on the floor, such as checkerboard or stripes. Or stencil to make the floor look like tiles.

PORCH SWING

You can never go wrong with adding a porch swing if your space allows it. If you'd prefer to buy something instead or make it yourself, there are plenty of options online, and throwing a few vibrant pillows on the swing adds instant charm.

TYPES OF PORCH DECKING

Choosing the materials for your porch floors can feel overwhelming. There are a wide variety of options based on your individual needs and aesthetic preferences. To choose the materials for your porch decking, consideration must be given to elements in your region and the amount of sun exposure your porch will receive.

Concrete may be a great option if your home is on a slab or only a few feet off the ground. It's a permanent and sturdy solution that can be stamped or stained to match your aesthetic.

Natural wood is another popular choice that's beautiful and simple to install. It does require maintenance as natural wood weathers easily with exposure to the elements. Every few years, you'll need to stain or paint wood decking to maintain its beauty. Redwood or cedar are great options that have natural properties that defend against rot, mold, and termites. If you live somewhere with high humidity and lots of rain, a tropical hardwood may be a great option. These woods are incredibly durable and can last for years.

Pressure-treated wood is a great option if you want the look of wood but want a lower-maintenance and lower-cost product that will remain decay-free for a minimum of fifteen years.

Synthetic decking is a man-made option that requires no upkeep to remain beautiful. Although it can be more expensive up front, in the long term, it can significantly save you time and money. Composite woods or plastics offer superior durability and resistance to rotting, staining, and splintering.

For our home, we chose to install pine boards from the trees we had felled from our property. We hired a portable sawmill company to cut the trees into slabs and then purchased a planer to transform them into boards. We then treated them with a pesticide, stickered and stacked them, and let them dry for a year. Once installed, we put a matte finish sealer on them. We will reseal them at least one time per year due to the intense sunshine we receive in Florida.

PORCH RAILINGS

Depending on your local building code, the height of your porches may require you to add a railing system, generally anything over 30 inches high. Our home starts at 60 inches high off the ground, so we were required to have railings on all our porches. The guardrail must be a minimum of 36 inches above the porch deck. On our front porch, we installed a system from a company called Viewrail. It's a modern system with wooden handrails, metal posts, and stainless steel rods. On our back porch, we simply used pressure-treated wood railings.

There are five main components to the handrail: posts, top rail, balusters, bottom rail, and top cap. If your home is off grade, handrailing posts are typically formulated into the overall design of your porch. Depending on the design and size of your porch, they could be either 4×4 or 6×6 posts. If your porch is lower to the ground, it may only be necessary to attach posts to the deck instead of anchoring them in the ground. This is typically done by cutting a 2-inch-deep by 6-inch-tall notch out of the bottom of your 4×4s and attaching them from the outside with the use of anchor bolts or headlock screws. If your house is slab on grade, handrailing is typically added for aesthetic purposes only, and the "posts" or anchor points will most likely be columns. Either way, these points are where you gain stability for your handrailing.

RAILING SYSTEMS

A system from a company like Viewrail is custom cut and designed for your exact layout. When the pieces arrive, you simply install using the layout guide they provide. The company projected this would take us about five days to complete, and we completed it in about three days.

They also provided every tool we needed, though we did make our own story pole, which allowed us to have a constant measurement for each pole without having to remeasure every time.

Project:

PORCH DECKING

Planning the spacing and layout of your porch decking will ensure you have a professional-looking final product.

Materials and tools needed:

tape measure
flooring material (measure
   deck area to determine
   quantities)
4-inch window tape, optional

Other tools as needed:

battery-powered impact driver
2 1/2-inch deck screws
miter saw
skill saw
jigsaw
table saw

Helpful steps for installing porch decking:

1. Carefully consider the layout and spacing of your boards. This may go without saying, but it's a good idea to check the framing of your deck to see if it's square. Take the time to measure and mark everything before installing your first piece.

2. Install window tape or zip tape over the top edge of floor joists, blocking, and all other flat surfaces that are below the decking to protect the wood from standing water and eventual decay. It adds to your cost, but it's a small price to pay to lengthen the life of your structure.

3. If you're installing deck boards in a horizontal pattern relative to your house, start installations with the decking boards farthest from the house and work your way toward your home. This will ensure that you have a full board at the end of the deck. If you start at the house and work out, there's a possibility that you'll end up with an unsightly, skinny rip all the way down the front edge of your deck, which you want to avoid. You can, however, start a full board at your house and work out. Using this method, there's obviously the risk of having the skinny cut at the end. To remedy this, prior to installing the decking, leave off your end rim joist. Once you get close enough, you can always trim floor joists back to accommodate the correct width (including the rim joist) for your final piece of decking.

4. To install wood decking, use either a hidden fastener system or attach directly through the face of your material. A hidden fastener system will create a cleaner aesthetic but will add additional time and costs to installation. Each fastener system has its own specifications, so be sure to follow the manufacturer's guidelines.

Project

PORCH RAILING

Handrailing can be as simple or decorative as you wish, but remember it will be exposed to the elements, so use only pressure-treated wood or weather-resistant products.

Materials and tools needed:

measuring tape
miter or skill saw
level
3-inch and 2.5-inch exterior
  screws
chalk box
post hole diggers
impact drill
jigsaw
framing square

Helpful steps for installing porch railing:

1. If your posts aren't already in place, cut new posts to desired height with your circular saw. If not anchoring them to the ground, notch the post as directed earlier, and install. Be sure posts are plumb and level with each progressive post.

2. Attach the top and bottom rail between the posts and on the inside edge closest to the home. The bottom rail should be a 2×4 installed horizontally on edge and start $3\frac{1}{2}$ inches above decking. Place a standard 2×4 on edge and use it as a gauge. The top rail should also be a 2×4 and will run horizontally between posts as well. The top of the top rail should be flush with posts.

3. After the top and bottom rails are securely attached with screws, start the install of your balusters. Balusters should be spaced evenly and not exceed 4-inch gaps between each baluster. The easiest way to achieve equal spacing is to again use a standard 2×4 ($3\frac{1}{2}$-inch width) as your gauge.

4. Attach the top cap. Most people use 2×4s for the top cap, but some prefer to use 2×6s. We chose to use a 2×6 top cap because it provided more surface area to lean on as well as a place to set drinks. You can also choose to router the edge of the top cap to provide a more finished look.

AFTERWORD

Pouring our hearts, blood, sweat, and tears to create the home of our dreams was something we thought would be a once-in-a-lifetime thing—something we created and then enjoyed for the rest of our lives. Somewhere we would gather for holidays for generations to come and tell the story of how we sacrificed everything to build the home everyone was now enjoying.

But as they say, "Tell God your plans, and He will laugh at you."

Rather than being an end to a dream, the conclusion of a lifelong aspiration, the journey that began while we were building turned this home into a stepping-stone along the way. It ignited a passion in us we knew was there, but we had no idea how deeply it was rooted. Rather than being an end to the journey, it was just the beginning.

That long-ago goal of Daniel's to build his own home with his own hands someday has now become a full-time career and something we are so excited to do again. All the knowledge we garnered, all the lessons we learned, and all the experience we acquired is now being put to use as we renovate newer homes and old farmhouses and plan another build of our own.

No matter where you are on your journey—whether it's just beginning to explore doing your own DIY projects, or you're ready to tackle a full-on, brand-new construction build—we hope you find inspiration from our journey. The ability to create a space you love, no matter how large or small the budget, is a truly amazing thing. And you never know—it may lead to fulfilling dreams you never even realized you had.

ACKNOWLEDGMENTS

To our children, while there have been blessings greater than we could have ever fathomed from this journey, we know that this entire process required sacrifices from every single one of you. We are forever grateful for your love, support, and patience as we worked tirelessly to provide you with the best life possible. Our hope is that through our journey, you learn to passionately and relentlessly pursue your dreams, not be afraid to do the hard work, and most importantly, know that anything worth having is worth fighting for.

To our parents, we could not have accomplished any of this without your support and love.

Bonnie Honeycutt, you are the most patient, understanding editor we could have ever asked for. Thank you for helping us create a cohesive, usable book out of all the chaotic knowledge in our heads.

Adria Haley, thank you for believing in us and for everything you did to make this book a reality.

Jenny Baumgartner, you are the reason for all of this—thank you, thank you, thank you!

Leslie Brown, thank you for capturing such gorgeous images of our home!

The rest of our Thomas Nelson team:

Tiffany Forrester, you did a fabulous job pulling all our pictures together into a beautiful book.

Kristen Sasamoto, thank you for all your work making sure our book was as lovely and functional as possible.

Marilyn Jansen, your guidance in editing was greatly appreciated.

Jennifer Gott, thank you for all your hard work in publishing our book.

Kristi Smith, we are so grateful for everything you did to help make our book a success!

ABOUT THE AUTHORS

Noell and Daniel Jett are the creative force behind the popular Jett Set Farmhouse, where they, along with their five children, share their lives, DIYs, cleaning and organization tips, recipes, homeschooling advice, and their home-building journey with their millions of followers. They are currently building their second farmhouse in Saint Augustine, Florida.